A Call from the Country

A CALL FROM THE COUNTRY

By

Kensinger Jones

And

Alice Guseman Jones

Library of Congress Catalog Card Number 88–051953

ISBN: 0–923568–02–6

Cover photo by Chuck Fedorowicz

PUBLISHED BY

Wilderness Adventure Books
320 Garden Lane
Box 968
Fowlerville, Michigan 48836

Manufactured in the United States of America

To our late parents, with deep appreciation:

Walter C. Jones
   A City Man who loved nature.

Anna Kensinger Jones
   Who made the best of it.

Sherman W. Guseman
   A fine farmer and countryman.

Mina Burton Guseman
   Who couldn't imagine any better life.

Contents

PREFACE

1   A PLACE IN THE COUNTRY   1
    Background – finding the land and why

2   HOW TO LOOK AFTER A LAKE   12
    First advisor – second advisor – deepening
    the shoreline – tragedy – catfish addition
    – leaking dam

3   SOME LESSONS IN LAND ACQUISITION   27
    Riparian rights – more acres – the survey

4   SOMEPLACE TO STAY   35
    The shack – the mobile home – the first
    party – the new house – house problems
    – satisfactions

5   DOUBLE LIVING, DOUBLE FUN   46
    Chicago weeks – country weekends – pro-
    jected projects – discovered pleasures –
    early visitors

6   ON MAKING A VERY MAJOR MOVE   58
    Decisions – Aurohn via Australia – the
    addition

7   ON BECOMING PART OF THE COMMUNITY   66
     Fall home tour — Great Books Club —
     county offices

8   ON NEIGHBORS   77
     Apartment vs. country neighbors — Charlie
     and his stories — the shadbush

9   TOOLS OF THE TRADE   91
     First tool box — motorized help — catas-
     trophes — ice storm — life without
     electricity

     MAPS AND PHOTOS   103

10   MAKING IT PAY   109
     Father's farm — new land plan — Aurohn
     farm

11   THE WOODS   122
     Nature's tabernacle — planned culling —
     tree farm

12   TREES   133
     Esthetic — practical

13   GROWING THINGS   141
     Daffodils — gardening — pests — additions
     and deletions

14   BRIDGING THE GENERATION GAP   159
     Friends' kids — their grandkids — their pets

15   FROM FARAWAY PLACES   169
     Australia – Malaysia – Singapore – China

16   GRANDPA'S FARM   184
     And grandkids

17   OWNERS OF ALL OUTDOORS   195
     Hoppers – swimmers – runners – climbers – crawlers – flyers – and us

18   DOUBTS, DILEMMAS, AND DECISIONS   208
     Writing – freelancing – teaching – adjustments

Preface

MANY PEOPLE live freeway lives, barreling along career and social paths without a moment's hesitation. Because most of us are happier traveling in pairs, there's generally someone along for the ride. Whether the companion is entirely happy is not the driver's concern. The mission is to reach some preconceived and defined destination, preferably together. Never mind the beckoning side road that might slow the journey, or indeed, lead to a place never imagined. Drive on.

This is the story of a detour, a rerouting of two lives at midpoint. The road changed and so, indeed, did the people who took it.

If these chapters suggest that you consider some alternate routes of your own, that there may be a happier way for you and your companion to travel together, good. Bumps there will be, times when you'll feel like turning back, questions, always. Chances are, though, that you'll pay a good deal more attention to each other as you move into new territory.

Acknowledge-
ments

Four people encouraged us to keep seeking publication:

Wilferd A. Peterson of Grand Rapids, Michigan
Jim and Rosalie Heacock of Santa Monica, California
Clayton Klein of Fowlerville, Michigan

We thank them.

For his assistance in the complexities of computer conversion, we also are grateful to:

Dr. Keith Adler, of Michigan State University

1

A Place in the Country

KEN:

THERE'S A REGULAR *chkkk, chkkk, chkkk* sound that means a squirrel is shucking a hickory nut somewhere in the foliage over your head. You stretch your neck back and back and look for one single flick of gray or red in the leaves. The sun plays tricks on you and everything goes to an orange haze. Actually, after a few minutes, a kind of dizziness takes you and you almost move. But you don't, because just the rustle of your feet and the game will be gone. Five minutes, almost, of concentration so intense the only thing in existence is a line of sight from you upwards to a nut clustered branch. A mosquito whines in, settles on your forehead, and drinks. Behind you a woodpecker beats a fast tattoo. Then, some shell peelings come tumbling down and you locate the branch, then the outline, the squirrel's head. You ease the twenty-gauge to your shoulder but before you can fire, some reflection, some unguarded move, alerts the bushytail. It whisks away, turns invisible. You lower the gun and breathe again. The hunter, the primitive game seeker inside you vanishes, too, magically, at least for the moment. The adrenalin subsides, the heartbeat slows, and the exhilaration is over.

In your hand it glistens like a jewel, shiny where you rubbed it on your corduroy pants. It's warm with the sun's warmth, and has a velvety feel. When you bite, the juice squirts into your mouth, acid, yet sweet. Careless, you feel the stickiness on your cheeks, the end of your nose, as you wolf it down. Nothing, anywhere, a la carte, on the dinner, or as a side, could taste this good. A fresh, ripe, really ripe, tomato out of your unkempt, but fully organic garden.

There's a kind of tiredness that's a pure blessing. It makes you understand the miracle of your own musculature, the fantastic fulcrums and levers that came with the package at birth. It's the end of a day in the country after a week in the city. It's dark after lighted hours of pure effort, lifting, climbing, digging, walking, bending, after countless commands to knees and fingers, feet and arms and beautiful obedience by every member. Now, rest earned, you seek sleep for the marvelous company that is yourself and you find it with crickets calling just outside. But before consciousness gives way to dreams you ask again, "How did I come here?" Press the rewind button. Run the reel back forty-five years. Look again at that unlikely beginning and blending.

Oil and water, dog and cat, mouse and elephant, town and gown, those are some of the classic confrontations. Rural and urban, city and country, are icons of conflict, too.

Maybe that's why our respective mothers were somewhat disturbed when they learned that Alice and I were launched on a love affair and heading towards marriage.

Alice's mother had the better reason. After all, I was a soldier, just returned from overseas, an unknown quantity, on temporary duty at Clarion State Teachers College. Outlanders of all kinds had descended on the small Pennsylvania school from which her daughter was about to graduate. Moreover, I was a city boy, probably worldly wise and sophisticated, an out-and-out slicker. Not at all the kind of man for a girl from a farm near Grindstone, Pennsylvania. That's what must have occurred to Mom Guseman when Alice wrote home about her new boy friend from St. Louis.

As for Mother Jones, the lady who had brought me into the world, she figured that I had been too long on duty in Alaska and the Aleutians and was therefore starved for romance. A pretty, little farmer's daughter had turned my head and I was, mama felt, likely to do something foolish. People should marry people from similar backgrounds. Marriage was tough enough when you started from a common base. Hasty matrimony, leisurely repentance and all that sort of thing. She urged me, by letter and phone, to be wary.

Despite these maternal insights, and well-meant warnings from both sides, the course of true love ran powerfully, recklessly, inevitably, during those World War II years. All sorts of odd couples were cementing relationships with wedding bands. G.I.'s brought home brides from England, Australia, France, Germany, from the Phillipines, Japan, India, China, everywhere. Massive cases of culture shock were commonplace as new realities impinged on rosy romance. America was a mixmaster. North, South, East, West, city, suburb, country, Protestant, Catholic, Jew, shake 'em all up and make a new nation, indivisible, with confusion, consternation and adjustment for all.

Love me now, know me later, let's get married, then we can get better acquainted. That was my story presented, in person, for five quick months. Then, a transfer ended the campus courtship and I continued the suit by correspondence from California, North Carolina and Mississippi. A delay enroute between postings got me to Grindstone and the farm, an awkward interview with her father, a fast trip with Alice to St. Louis to meet my family. She wore an engagement ring home.

Our parents could not but run with the tide. They reluctantly cooperated as we planned our own unlikely marriage. From Brownsville, in southwestern Pennsylvania, diminutive Alice, just graduated with a degree in library science, made her way, by train to St. Louis.

Simultaneously, I, on the verge of discharge from the U.S. Army Infantry, got ten days' leave and headed North from Camp

Shelby, Mississippi. Meanwhile, my resigned mother made arrangements for church, minister and reception in our old neighborhood. We, the happy couple, arrived separately in Union Station just hours apart, she from the East, I from the south. We scrambled for blood tests and license, and were united in matrimony about thirty hours later.

It had been a little less than a year since my buddy, Artie Jaquess and I walked into the Clarion State College Book Store and I glimpsed this pert and pretty person behind the counter.

"Artie," I proclaimed, "I'm going to marry that girl."

Ahead of us stretched the rest of our lives to compare backgrounds, value systems, and to work out the riddle of mutual happiness. City boy, country girl, where do you go now?

You go where the work is and the work turns out to be advertising. First stop, St. Louis, then aboard the career coach for Chicago, Detroit, Sydney, Singapore, with occasional stints in New York, Hollywood, Nashville, Dallas, wherever the will-o-wisp of a writing vocation might lead. Pack up the suitcases, load the furniture, hit the road and don't forget the kids and pets. Make new friends, entertain the bosses, join the PTA, have an open house and meet the new neighbors. Don't look back, Alice, except once or twice a year when we'll whiz homeward to the farm for Thanksgiving or family reunion.

The country folk nod politely as we regale them with our farflung adventure stories, show slides of palaces, pyramids and port cities, ships, chateaus and show biz people.

"When will they ever settle down?" the home folks wonder.

For a few days, for the interlude of a week or two, Alice recaptures the wonderful, slower rhythm of life as she knew it for her first twenty years. Deliberate conversations about unimportant things like weather, relatives, weddings, births and deaths, take place on the pendulum of a porch swing. Our children run free in a field of corn stubble, pick up apples from the orchard ground, ride bareback on old Dude.

I help with the haying or threshing, the corn harvest or milk bottling, and wonder what's happening at the office. My back aches and my legs are tired from unwonted effort and exercise, but I've proven I can put in as good a day's work as the old hands and have blisters on mine to prove it.

It's good to get back to the office in Chicago or Detroit, where people have to keep up with me rather than the vice-versa of farm time. Alice gets out the lists of who-we-owe and who-owes-us and reconstructs our social calendar. Each succeeding home, in whatever city, is a bit bigger and in a better neighborhood. Each party is a bit more elaborate. I'm having the time of my life, clambering skillfully over the monkey bars of executive progression. Alice, kids in tow, is adept and adaptable and keeps up womanfully.

Occasionally I break away from the city for a few days of trout fishing with business buddies, hunting with a client or two, even a long weekend at a lake resort with just the family. That's the country I truly love, a place for rest and rehab, but not too much of it.

Usually a couple of reports, some scripts and a writing assignment go along in a brief case to be read by the soft, yellow glow of the kerosene lamp while Alice and our boy and girl play Hearts.

Then, suddenly, the children are grown. The suburban house in Huntington Woods, just outside of Detroit, is much too big. The executive game turns stale, the work wearisome, even in a four-window office.

Imagine a room forty feet long and twenty wide, with floor length drapes of muted green and ochre, with a massive desk and cadenza, a motion picture projection set-up, a three piece sofa and big circular coffee table. Occupy it with six serious men, mostly in their thirties and forties. Their coats are off, the coffee cups are drained, the ash trays need emptying. It's long past closing time but they haven't even talked about adjourning. The floor is strewn with the wreckage of a million dollars worth of advertising. Storyboards for commercials that will never be shot. Finished artwork and carefully measured and set type for magazine ads that will never rest between the covers of *Life* and

Reader's Digest and *McCall's*. Discarded newspaper advertisements line the wall ledges.

This is an army of brain children suddenly miscarried, destroyed before being born. The labor pains spanned four months and the baby never had a chance.

"We've changed our minds," the client said, "the product's not ready to put on the market, so you'll just have to put the advertising campaign on the back burner. What I need right now is some hard-hitting clean-up advertising for the lines that are in the stores. I want to see something in a couple of days."

So six men plan and work, trying to kindle some kind of spark from the ashes of a sensless little catastrophe that in its way seems as mindless and devastating as a hurricane. Egos are crushed, vacations are postponed and the very structure of the agency seems threatened. The tired professionals work to mend and fix and save, and the morning newspaper trucks are on the street before we all go home.

This kind of tiredness is almost illness. The brain keeps probing, searching, looking for reasons where there are none. The body stays tense and stray tremors move restively in the cheek, the calf, across the chest. It's been months, years, maybe, since you could let it all go, since you could slide off to slumber like a canoe sliding down a bank and into a lake. Even the old images of peaceful water and star-crossed skies don't help anymore, nor does the aspirin or the brandy shot.

Something has to change. You must shake the old house down and build a new one, and in the new one there has to be a place to rest. A place with fish in the water and squirrels in the trees and tomatoes on the vine in the garden. The idea has been there all along. It was why you went on those camping trips in the Michigan woods and the high desert country of Wyoming. It was the magnet that each year took the family back to the Pennsylvania farm.

It was A Place In The Country. All you had to do was find it.

With executive cunning you delegated the job to that resident expert on things rural, your wife.

ALICE:

Ken was fifty; and a long power struggle had ended in defeat. There followed a new corporate challenge, but his heart wasn't in it. When you've been within inches of the top of a mountain and then had to turn back, the next climb looks tougher. He needed something to restore a bruised and battered spirit. So we talked. My sympathetic, but somewhat frustrated questioning, finally elicited an answer that changed our lives.

Me: "Well, what *would* you like?"

He: "I'd like a little corner of the world where I could be all alone . . . and fish anytime I wanted to." (Said plaintively and requiring a warm and wifely answer.)

Me: "O.K. While you're digging into your new job I'll find something."

Such nonchalant confidence! In my ignorance I thought that if my father, and his father before him, could acquire their very own farms, we could easily find a few acres. Then I started to learn about rural real estate.

Like a beagle searching for a warm scent, I ranged in all directions. Taking to the trail of a morning in my new Cutlass, with Robin, my faithful poodle for company, I would track down the places glowingly described in the real estate section of the daily paper. So many muddy lanes in which to get stuck. So many winding roads to lost, dead ends. So many high hopes fanned by phone conversations assuring me, "There's a lovely woods and a fine fishing place." So many scraggly groves and uncertain trickles full of tin cans.

Then there were the prices. This was *before* the great Real Estate Boom. Rural property was often priced at $100 to $200 an acre. That is, until a city buyer appeared.

Twenty acres, nice, small home, ideal for horses—$7500.

Shocking! Especially since the acres were scrub and swamp, the small house a shack, and horses would have been hard put to find enough grass to stay alive.

And water! Anything with a spot damp enough to breed a

mosquito was at least $1,000 an acre. Totally exorbitant. Hope kept springing eternal, encouraged by more classified ads.

FOR SALE:

> 120 acres of partially wooded land. Ideal for Hunting Club.
> Within one hour of downtown.

This one I didn't even mention to Ken. His early enthusiasm for my search was flagging, especially as he calculated the costs of becoming a country gentleman. This time I went to the real estate company that had signed the ad and asked if there was any water on the place. The realtor said he thought that was a possibility. He'd never visited the acreage. Fortunately the two old gentlemen who were the owners were expected in that morning, so I waited for them. They were the brothers Zyblinski and they had a great deal to say to each other, entirely in their native tongue. Since the realtor and I spoke only English, which they failed to comprehend, it confined communication to pleasant smiles and nods. Obviously none of my questions could be answered, so the realtor suggested that we all drive down and look at the place.

Encouraged by the possibility of a creek, a spring, or some sort of aquatic opportunity, I agreed.

I demurred, however, from accompanying the owners in their pickup truck and simply followed them down the expressway, past the outskirts of Detroit for miles, and miles and miles, through Monroe and out the other side onto some secondary roads. An hour and a half later, signaling indicated we were nearing the property, and we turned off onto a dirt road.

Water was what I was looking for and, suddenly, there it was. A few warm days had melted heavy snows. It had flooded vast expanses of absolutely flat land that stretched away in every direction like a foot-deep Lake Michigan. In the distance, a line of scraggly trees reached dejectedly up from the morass. Driving further seemed a little much to ask of a lady, her dog and a compact car. I tooted, waved and turned back but not before watching for a moment as the truck splashed majestically into the sunset like an ancient amphibian heading for its den. The price was $500 an acre.

FOR SALE

Country acreage. Ideal for building. Adjoins State Park.
Forty-five minutes from Detroit, just off the freeway.

Didn't sound too bad. I looked. And found the "just off the freeway" was about thirty feet, and the State Park entrance was right across the road. What really turned me off was the budding garden of non-returnable beer can tops peeking through the melting snow. Evidently either people entering the park stopped and had a few before proceeding, or dumped their litter on the way out. That land, because it was so accessible, could be had for $1,000 an acre.

Since two months of trying traditional methods hadn't worked and I was getting discouraged, I did something outlandish.

First, I must explain that I like the radio, especially those programs in which people phone in to air their views, even when those views are as wild as the Red Queen's. I like interviews with famous people from Paul Newman and Jeff Bridges to Eleanor Smeal, George Schultz, and Paul Harvey. Those voices are company in a solitary world of inanimate objects like unwashed dishes, unmade beds, and undone laundry. Those voices are nice to have along as I try to convert chaos into order. Those voices are nice in the *car*.

At the time this all happened, I was a great fan of Detroit's Station WTAK, called Double-U Talk. They broadcast eighteen hours a day of pure conversation. One of their morning shows was "Tradio". It invited listeners who needed things to phone in, state their needs and hope for a response from someone in the radio audience. Mostly the calls were about bicycles for trade, second-hand refrigerators, sets of encyclopedias and outgrown clothing.

It was at the car wash where muddy evidence of one morning's fruitless search was being removed, that I heard the day's first caller. A woman wanted to buy a second-hand collapsible baby buggy for twins. Our needs couldn't be that unusual, I gloomily reflected. So, on arriving home, I marched immediately to the phone and was suddenly on the air.

"What I'm looking for is a place on a lake or stream for my husband. It should be within an hour's drive of the city and something that can be stocked if it hasn't fish already. He wants to fish. It should be isolated, so it will be a good retreat, and it shouldn't be too expensive. If you know of such a place call LIncoln 8-4307."

The M.C. of the show was a little stunned.

"That's an unusual request," he told his audience, and went on to the next call.

Fifteen minutes later, over the noise of the vacuum, I heard the phone ring. It was Mrs. Harb. Her husband had a lake he wanted to sell. It was full of fish, and a little more than an hour from the city. Would Mrs. Jones want to look at it?

I certainly did! The next Saturday, with directions given me by phone, dog and I hit the road again. Actually, it was a good two hours' drive from the city, and Mr. Harb's lake was seven miles from Hastings, Barry County's picture-book seat of government.

The last three miles were on bone-jarring narrow gravel roads. Even through a couple of inches of snow you could feel the bumps and the promise of potholes come the spring thaw. Finally we slid to a stop and I read the sign "Pritchardville Road". It was a cold, grey day and we'd been lost twice and it was much farther from home than we wanted it to be. But—this wasn't flat, tame country. Across the road it fell away sharply, and there were wooded hills meeting the scudding snow on the other side of a narrow valley.

My spirits took an upward swing. I turned right, according to instructions, went half-a-mile, then a hundred yards past a white farm house, pulled the car over and got out. Little dog jumped out and promptly disappeared in a drift. I picked her up and carried her.

"Walk about fifty yards," Mr. Harb had said over the phone, "towards some twin maples. Between them you'll see the lake."

There it was, or it's outline at least. The water was locked beneath a foot of ice and snow was drifted on top of that. It was much bigger than I had imagined. There was no sound, no movement, except the wind and the snow, and a rising excitement within me. Back in the car I turned on the engine, started the heater, and thought, "It's probably too far away, and I don't know what it costs, but if it's solitude and beauty we want, this is it." Turning carefully to avoid drifts and ditches, we started back toward the big city.

Three weeks later, without checking the tax situation, running a survey, haggling, investigating the area, or consulting local realtors, we bought the place for Mr Harb's full asking price. In due course, we had problems over an inaccurate abstract, mistaken titles, exorbitant tax increases. We learned that the price had been kited and we'd paid more per acre than anybody else around. But the hunch was right. The search was over and something great had happened in our lives. We were about to get back to basics.

About six weeks later, Station WTAK changed its call letters and became an all-music station. We hated to see that happen. *Talk* had brought us the end of a rainbow—cheap! And Ken had his lake.

Life might continue turbulent. My husband would probably steam along, as always, on some career course or other, with me somewhere in the wake. But, thankfully, we now, occasionally, could anchor in a peaceful pool, rest together, before rejoining the Success-Bound Convoy.

Or so it seemed.

2

How to Look After a Lake

KEN:

BARRY COUNTY, MICHIGAN, has been referred to as "the only upper peninsula county in the lower peninsula." There are only some 40,000 people living on its 575 square miles and most of them are in three or four towns. There are three hundred lakes, thousand of acres of swamp and woodland. It's surrounded by fair-sized cities, Grand Rapids, Kalamazoo, Lansing and Battle Creek, and is only two hours from Detroit.

What it doesn't have are four-lane, crowded highways, huge resort complexes, and heavy promotion. It's a kind of private place with a lot of private people. It likes the way it is, and is in no hurry to get on with the twenty-first, or even the twentieth century. Alice had found us a lake in a land that time might not have forgotten, but it certainly wasn't pushing for "progress."

Paradise, unspoiled, is what we thought we bought.

But, as we discovered, man and his clutter aren't the only problems. There's Mother Nature, the old harridan, and her tricks and turns. Leave her alone and she'll give you a bumper crop of thornapple trees, acres of waterweeds, stout cables of Virginia creeper and wild grapes to choke your walnut trees to death. She'll supply stunted fish and murdered ducks. That's just for starters. If she takes a notion, she can snap off foot-thick branches with an ice storm, punch a hole in a dam with a lightning bolt, smother a thousand finny swimmers with a capricious temperature change. All in all my experience has taught us to look on her as the most liberated and antagonistic female around. Scratch the Mother, and call her Madame.

The first intimation we had that we were embarking on a long term contest with the Old Lady came from John Hamp. John represented the Barry County Soil Conservation District. You might say he was the voice of the U.S. Department of Agriculture when it came to Land Use.

We asked him to come out and help us plan a program for our new ninety acres with the twenty-acre lake in the middle. It was very early spring. The ice was gone, except for a few crystal clusters clinging to the dam overflow and at little inlets along the shore line. It was a cold, brilliant day and the three of us were standing on the hill where the lake ended. We had walked over a good piece of the property, and Alice and I were feeling pretty great. A thousand plans were bubbling in our respective brains. John lit his pipe.

"Well," he asked, "what do you want it to be?"

Little waves danced across the blue water. The hill on the other side held a hint of green, and a dark row of pines marched across its base.

"Just like it is," I answered, and then a little copywriter boiled over. "A sanctuary for birds and game, an unspoiled place, a small wilderness."

Alice nodded agreement.

John Hamp had spent his life coping with the vagaries of land, water and weather and with the minor insanities of man. He hated to see denuded hills where sheep had grazed too long because of an owner's greed. He was equally irritated by lake banks broken down by uncontrolled muskrats. He fervently believed that man's intelligence is a proper part of the natural world.

"Just like it is is the one thing it can't be," he said. "Not five minutes from now or five years from now. It can't even be exactly whatever you decide you want for it. But, if you start now, you might come close."

Since that time John has retired to what I hope is a better-ordered world. His words go marching on. We make our plans, effect them, and about the time we become self-congratulatory, zingo . . . the Old Lady comes through with a trick or two of her own. Just take the lake itself, about a quarter-mile long, and maybe two-hundred yards wide. Twenty feet deep at its deepest. There are times when it seems as big as the Atlantic and as uncontrollable as Niagara, as cruel as the Arctic Ocean or as beneficent as Warm Springs. It's everything Water can be, delicious and threatening, sustaining and destroying, domestic and wild.

It's quite young as lakes go, having been created about thirty years ago by two fishermen from Chicago. John Hamp, himself, had told them that their idea of a dam at the end of a narrow valley was impractical. So impractical that Conservation Department funds, available at the time to assist in setting up water reservoirs, were denied them. The tiny stream that piddled through the valley was inadequate, there just wasn't enough water supply.

"Forget it," John told them.

So they built it anyway. And this time the Old Lady did something nice. Hidden underground, at the head of the valley, was a bountiful spring. As the water rose slowly, muskrats came to what was, essentially, a swamp. They tunneled and dug and nested, and gradually opened the spring. The water found its way to the surface. The little stream ran faster and the lake filled within a year. "The boys," as John called them, stocked it with bass and bluegill, and within three years they were catching three-pound bass anytime they wanted, bluegills the size of saucers, bright orange sunfish, and a few crappies that had mysteriously appeared. For half-a-dozen years things got better and better.

Then Madame Nature had a tantrum. One night she threw an electrical wingding and sent a million-volt bolt crashing into the spillway. It followed along the galvanized steel drain pipe at the bottom of the dam and tore out a hole two feet in diameter. Water pumped out like blood from a punctured artery. Luckily a neighbor heard a roaring sound and within a few hours a bulldozer was on hand to apply a massive dirt tourniquet and shut off the flow that was almost fatal.

By that time a lot more than water had spurted out. The valley below the dam was alive with floundering, flopping, gasping fish. Wagonloads of them. Dozens of dozens were scooped up, carried up the hill and put back in the impoundment. Hundreds and hundreds expired. Slowly the lake refilled, reached back up to the top of the spillway. The Old Lady giveth and, when the mood's upon her, she taketh away.

Of course, that was all history the day the three of us stood on the hill. Our own involvements were just beginning. As far as the lake was concerned, John promised to send us some pamphlets with titles like *Weed Control in Michigan Lakes, How to Attract Waterfowl* and *Building Wood Duck Nests*. He gave us the names of some fisheries folks. He suggested we seek more specialized advice than he could give us.

"Heck," he said, "I'd have guessed there'd never be a lake here at all. And look."

It was late enough in the day so that pink was appearing in the west and reflecting in the far end. Alice and I looked at each other. A few months ago we'd never have guessed we'd be here at all, either. We started back for the car.

The next man to analyze the lake had astonishing credentials. His most recent assignment had been a visit to Lake Victoria in Africa for consultation on measures to control an aquatic snail whose parasitic activities were hazardous to human life. Before that he'd been to Vietnam's Mekong Delta to advise on some dam-building activities. He was a department head at the University of Michigan and also operated a separate consulting service.

We heard about him at a cocktail party. One of the other guests had owned a place with a completely contained lake not far from the University at Ann Arbor. Their department of environmental education had agreed to use this little lake as a laboratory for graduate students. Gratis, they'd cleared it of weeds, stocked it with fish, improved it as habitat and done other wonderful things. Visions of stalwart, tanned students improving my place danced through my head. So I wrote to the Expert.

He wrote back. My location was too far from Ann Arbor for it to be a University project site. However, in his role as an independent consultant, he'd be glad to take a look at it, help me plan to maximize its potential. His rate for the consulting was three hundred dollars a day, plus the cost of transportation. I was staggered. But, I thought, I'll never have another lake. He should be able to case the place in a couple of hours, or one-twelfth of three hundred is around twenty-five bucks and transportation shouldn't be more than another twenty, and why not, anyhow.

We conducted some more vague negotiations by letter and phone, and finally, made a date.

By this time I figured the experience and advice should cost me about a hundred dollars, and there was still the outside chance that he *would* pick it up for a graduate student project.

Because our stays at the place were almost exclusively on weekends, it had to be a Sunday when the Expert arrived. It was the kind of Sunday when nobody should be in church and everybody should be outside worshiping the God who put it all together. It was maybe seventy-two degrees, the air was so clear it crackled, and the woods were at least fifteen shades of gorgeous green.

We strolled the banks. He had a stick which he'd poke into the shoreline mud. He studied the rushes and other plants. He stared into the water and examined the face of the dam. He watched some swallows skim the surface and we were both delighted when three mallards flapped up out of a marsh. I contained my usual garrulousness because he seemed to be thinking and, for the price, I certainly didn't want to interfere. After more than an hour we sat on some camp stools and talked.

He is an apostle of aquarius, a water wizard, a man completely absorbed in the world of H_2O. He is an optimist and believes that man can reverse the ruinous pollution of ocean, stream and lake. He is a naturalist and believes that we must proceed with caution when it comes to dams. reservoirs, dikes and other man-made impediments to natural flow and natural habitat. He thinks aqua pura is *the* great treasure a man can have and made me understand that what I had acquired through a real estate deal was worth far more than whatever I had paid per acre.

"It also," he said, "will be worth a lot of money to your heirs. A recreational area with good water this close to the big cities has got to be a gold mine. If you can buy more land like this, buy it. To tell the truth, I envy you."

That's a nice vote of confidence in the lake if ever I heard one.

Along with it he suggested some projects. Make it deeper. Protect the dam. Own it all. Most of all, though, said the Expert, enjoy it. Don't get obsessed with "finishing" things. If you're shoveling, don't forget to look at the sky. If you can't complete something by fall, don't sweat it, spring is on the way. Water is a ceaseless wonder so let it entertain as well as occupy you.

He said he'd send us some advisory notes, and his bill. That was fifteen years ago, and they haven't arrived yet. If he reads this, I hope he'll contact us, come see us again when he returns from the Amazon or Orinoco, the Dnieper or Rhine or Nile or Yukon, from the Yellow Sea, the Bay of Fundy or whatever place he may be.

I hate being in debt, and I'd love to see him again.

He had suggested deepening the lake. We decided to follow his advice along the north shoreline not imagining that we'd trigger two ecological catastrophes. All we intended was to create a channel, five to six feet deep, where there'd be no weeds, where a boat could navigate easily, and where we might create three little islands where ducks could loaf.

All that was needed was a bull dozer and a drag line. They could be hired. Obviously, however, before we could do any deepening, we'd have to lower the water level by opening the spillway. Simple. I could do that myself.

Now our spillway is a little unusual. It's like a small elevator shaft. Water comes in over the top and drops eighteen feet to a pipe that carries it under the dam and so down the valley. On three sides the shaft is solid concrete. The fourth side is a series of 6" × 52" × 1½" boards that can be pulled one at a time to lower the lake . . . one board out and the lake is lowered six inches at the spillway.

Imagine yourself doing it. You stand in water in hip boots. You pry loose a board swollen by ten years of soaking. As a crack opens, the water rushes through, making it hard for you to stand. It's backbreaking, slow, like building pyramids or setting up stone chimneys, like all the work our grandfathers and theirs did to make things happen. You lose track of time, and you feel like the king of the world when you move two boards a day. It's a feeling you don't get in an office, even when you help bring in a new account or sell a good campaign. The next morning you see a rim of mud where the water has receded. It looks like the ring around a giant bathtub.

The lowering took twelve weeks. Now there was a broad brown margin around the whole circumference. It was November. There would be maybe a month before the ground froze, a month for the dragline to deepen the channel. Then the lake would lie low all winter, and, in the spring the dozer could level up the shoreline. It was all working beautifully.

Except for one thing. The balance of nature had been dealt a rude and shocking blow. As the film of ice formed, and the snow blanketed the earth scars, there was no evidence that murder had been done. That came with the spring thaw.

It was a day in March when we walked the shoreline and saw the tragedy. First one big bullfrog, maybe fourteen inches long. He seemed to be crouched on the bottom in a few inches of water. He didn't move when we stirred him with a stick. He was dead. Then, another, two feet further along . . . and another and dozens and dozens, mute victims of an event they couldn't cope with. The frogs, you see, had gone into hibernation before the lake was fully lowered.

The insulation that kept them from freezing was water, a couple feet of it, and it had been drained away while they slept. The icy hand of winter had reached down and taken their lives from them.

The second cataclysm came almost as an anti-climax.

It was a month or so later, when the water had begun to warm. Suddenly fish began to float to the surface and wash ashore. Two and three pound bass. Bluegills. Sunfish. Dozens, first, and finally hundreds. When we lowered the water level, we created shallows where they were stranded and finally suffocated as ice cut off the air supply. Fish, surprisingly, need oxygen as much as people.

So, we learned.

One nice thing about the Old Lady of the Outdoors is her capacity for healing after she injures. Eventually the dredging was done. Some frogs did survive and by the following year we were enjoying incredible early spring symphonies.

*Crrrrrunk . . . gulunnnnnnnk . . .*a single baritone frog would go at one end of the lake. He was the choir master.

Catateee . . . catateeeee . . . catateee . . . a hundred other alto and soprano frogs responded in chorus from our western swamp.

Beautiful music indeed.

And, a month after the mass murders, I caught a respectable bass, another and another. In the deeper holes, a sizable population hung in there.

"In the long run," a conservationist told me, "you made the lake a better place by the draining and deepening. In fact, some day you may have to do it again." I fervently hope not.

The memory of all those corpses haunted us even though nothing is wasted in nature. The baby hand prints of numerous raccoons, the strident calls of crows, and an occasional sighting of opossums and foxes explained the rapid disappearance of the mordant fish and frogs.

Concerned as she was about our losses, Alice was understandably struck by a small notice in the local Agriculture and Conservation Service mailing piece.

For Distribution: Fingerling bass, bluegill or channel catfish.
Contact the ASC Office.

She made an executive decision. We would not only replace some of the lost fish, but we would also expand the variety of fish for our avid angler friends.

She's chronicled the details of what became quite an involved transaction.

ALICE:

First came the garbage can. One of the instructions we received after placing our order was to have a twenty-gallon can of fresh, unchlorinated water into which the fish could be transferred. We bought a big new one, (never can have too many garbage cans), and I even scrubbed that out. Then we discovered that it wouldn't fit in the trunk of the family car. But it would in Ken's company-owned station wagon. We would trade vehicles for the day.

I got up extra early on the appointed morning, got the house and family organized, and started out, allowing three hours for the drive. This gave me an extra hour to allow for any minor problem in finding the post office in the little town of Nashville where the fishtank truck was scheduled to distribute orders at 11:30 A.M. The lovely, new station wagon purred down the six-lane expressway, tempting me to ignore the posted speed limit of 55 M.P.H . . . and occasionally succeeding. It was a beautiful day, a perfect time to install new residents into the lake. Fun!

Ten miles onto the limited access ribbon of concrete an evil red light glowed at me from the dash. The engine heating up? . . . on this new car? At the third stop to replace the rapidly evaporating water, a trained mechanic diagnosed and replaced the faulty thermostat. Forty-five minutes had been lost and I was so intent on making up for lost time that I sailed right through Nashville before realizing I'd arrived. Finding the post office, I questioned an outdoorsy looking man leaning against a truck. He was waiting for his fish delivery also.

Hooray! There was time to fill the can with twenty gallons of water. Quickly going back to a service station two blocks away, I found an attendant who, after hearing my story, obligingly reached for the water hose. Laughingly I asked,

"You don't chlorinate your water here, do you?"

He slowly lowered the hose. In this little town they did! I was eyeing the little stream that was running back of the station, and wondering how long it would take to scoop up twenty gallons when he said, "I've a neighbor who has the only working fresh water well in town."

Armed with directions, I zipped across town again to find the house. It was locked.

There was a note on the door "Gone to dinner." Looking desperately around I noticed two curious spectators . . . a darling white-haired couple slowly rocking on their porch swing. Galloping up to them, I poured out my story. The gentleman gallantly helped me find an outside faucet and a hose at The-House-With-A-Well. With an optimism I didn't feel, I promised my cohorts to be back to show them the fish.

The run back across town was a bit more gingerly executed because of the twenty gallons of sloshing water. I got to the post office just in time to hear a man call out to the covey of spectators from the top of the conservation truck, "Is there anyone else before I leave?"

Leaping out of the car and waving my card, I presented myself breathlessly. It all seemed so anti-climactic, somehow, to be given a little bucket half full of wiggling two inch catfish to dump into the "twenty gallons of fresh, pure, water." When he said,

"There's about 750 there," I muttered, "I don't think I'll count them today!" . . . but thanked him most heartily, particularly for being an hour late.

With a real feeling that I'd accomplished the impossible, I again called the old couple to view the little fish. When they said they had a tiny pool in their back yard, I grandly presented them with six of the whiskered wigglers to put in it. At that moment the owners of The-House-With-A-Well returned and were delighted to hear the story of which they were unwittingly the heroes.

A gay wave and I set off on the final leg of my journey to the lake. Finally I could drive slowly and cautiously and *relaxed*. It was a real pleasure to anticipate the future when these tiny things would be big "sporting" fish, giving our fishing friends a thrill and eating some of the too-abundant waterweeds.

I drove as close to the edge of the lake as I dared. After gingerly pouring out enough water to make it manageable, I dragged the can to the edge of the dock. Our neighbor's young daughter was as excited as I when the can tipped over and the little fellows swam out into their new home. To our horror we watched three of them beset by angry resident fish. They floated away, belly-up. The rest darted for hiding places among the weeds along the edge of the water. Surely, a few will survive, I devoutly hoped!

At least one did. Ten years after the planting, because of a winter freeze-out, the body of a three foot, fourteen pound catfish washed ashore. When Ken brought home that poor, defunct creature for me to view, it warmed my heart. Because, useless as it was, it still meant success. If there was one, there had to be more. It signified the worth of a project undertaken and accomplished. That's important, especially when it has to do with my husband's original concept of country living. What we had, in our acres, fulfilled my long-dormant girlhood dream. I wanted to be sure that the lake also lived up to his fishing fantasies. I wanted him to be happy. However, as he found more and more to do, it became increasingly apparent that he wasn't about to be relaxed.

KEN:

Maybe so. I *did* worry about erosion, so we faced the dam with fieldstone and ran a log boom the length of it to stop the chewing effect of wind-driven water. We learned, in the process, that popple logs sink when water soaked and have to be replaced with hard woods.

A campaign of chemical warfare was launched on weeds around the beach area. Alice demurred because of danger to the young willows we had planted. One of them turned rather brown for a summer but fought its way back to health. From then on we dealt with the cattails by pulling them out bodily, one at a time.

It's alive, that lake, and I'm glad it tolerates my fooling with its face. It's alive, and like any living thing, it can fall ill. For more than fifteen years it was essentially quite healthy, and we never worried about its projected longevity.

Then came a drought, the worst in at least a decade. At first, we paid it little attention. Previously, in even the driest weather, the water had never fallen more than two or three inches. But in this summer season, July saw the level drop half-a-foot and, in August, yet another six inches.

There was nothing charming, now, about the musical sound of water tumbling down the spillway. It was an alarm sound, rather, that told us Aurohn Lake was bleeding dangerously. Water wasn't going out over the top, as intended. It was seeping out between the very boards designed and installed to hold it back. Age and rot were having their way. Alice applied band aids in the form of heavy plastic bags which she lowered into position by long sticks. The water flow and force pushed them against the cracks. One or two spots would be plugged, but only temporarily. A week later the bandages would have washed away.

We could no longer reassure ourselves by believing that a week of good, hard rain would bring the waterline back up where it belonged. The drought had revealed something systemic that needed correction. It proved to be a blessing, disguised.

By now the float boat that had always ridden buoyantly beside the dock was mired in mud. The moat around our tiny island was quite dry. Every day rivulets fingered their way between cracks in the spillway boards and left by the quart, the gallon, the tubful. When a surface that covers twenty acres goes down an inch, that's a lot of liquid. It was time to call for help and we did.

Two people from the Agricultural Stabilization and Conservation office came out to have a look. They mulled and talked. Thirty years, they said, was about as long as wood in an overflow could be expected to last. Ours was right on the edge of its expectancy. So what were the possible solutions?

We could pull all the boards and drain the lake. That would mean a gradually increasing sea of mud and trauma for all the frogs, turtles, snakes, ducks, geese, herons and salamanders who made their homes in the marshy margins. There would be thousands of fish gasping and flopping in sudden shallows, and ugliness for a year or two.

Or we could, our advisors suggested, build a coffer dam and divert the water to an emergency spillway while making necessary repairs. Hundreds of hours and thousands of dollars would be involved. We gulped at the prospect, but the dam had to be saved.

Then along came Dean Hill.

He loves the place like we do. His canoe, sometimes, lives on our shoreline. He brings best friends and neighbor kids and takes them fishing at sunset. He likes to watch their pleasure as the bluegills bite and the surface of the lake turns golden. Dean has done many difficult tasks for us, and he's done them all well. From the stone that crowns our chimney to the tile floor in the gunroom, to the new toolshed and the woodbox, his handiwork attests to his integrity. So, when he heard about the threat to the dam, he took it as a personal challenge.

With the crisis still upon us, we had to leave on a long-planned trip. The day we returned, two weeks later, Dean's old truck was parked beside the garage. He wasn't in sight, anywhere.

But he showed up about half-an-hour after our arrival. His

black hair dripped, sleek as an otter's fur. His muscled torso glistened wet and his ragged denim shorts were soaked through.

"I'm working on the dam," he announced.

By ladder, he had descended the twelve-foot deep overflow and, with water cascading over him, had devised a plan and was putting it into operation. It required sheets of heavy fibreglass wedged against the back of the old boards. That had been accomplished. Now he needed a co-worker and I was elected. For most of a day we worked. I sawed wood and handed it down to him in the narrow chimney with its constant shower. He shoved and wedged and jammed and gradually a new wall arose from the bottom supported by stout braces.

For awhile we weren't sure it would work. Pressure on the lower boards seemed to push the leaks higher. Finally, though, we were to the top and, while there was still leakage, it was dramatically reduced.

We dug clay and hauled it to the spillway in buckets. We plastered it against the boards, packed and pushed it until it sealed. The leaks became trickles and then drips.

The tourniquet had been applied and the bleeding stopped.

The lake was saved.

Thank God.

Thanks, Dean.

Since his pragmatic engineering operation we've had another dry spell. It has been referred to as "the drought of the century." Our lake dropped a foot, then eighteen inches. It stopped dropping when it reached the top of Dean's fibreglass wall.

In the evenings, sometimes, we walk along the water's edge, down to the dam, and then up a little rise just below it. From there you can see the expanse of water stretching nearly a quarter of a mile to the west where the hills fold it in. With the sunlight bouncing off the water and bathing her face, Alice looks like a pussy cat about to purr. She pays practically no attention as I comment on the slow growth of some of the pines we planted on the north slope. She doesn't seem to hear me when I point out places where muskrats have burrowed into the shore line. My plans to brush-hog below the dam don't seem to interest her. Eventually I fall silent, too, and, the next thing you know we're holding hands and watching two mallards swoop into the cove below us.

3

Some Lessons in Land Acquisition

KEN:

FOR YEARS, as the male head of the family, I considered myself the practical part of a pair. The romantic and sentimental were Alice's departments. Hers to remember birthdays, send appropriate anniversary cards, and exclaim over the uniqueness of any newly arrived baby born to friend or relative. Mine to balance the checkbook, negotiate with plumbers and carpenters, pick the new car. So tradition dictated and so we lived. But, as we got back to the land, lines began to blur.

One day, for instance, Alice brought up the question of riparian rights, a phrase I didn't know she knew.

Understand that when we bought the lake, we thought it was all, every beautiful drop of it, ours. That was certainly the impression we got from the seller. We were too entranced with the idea of being not just land, but water, owners to fool around with surveys, titles or other legal documents. That could all come later.

Spring came first and with it tender green grass and, immediately thereafter, a flock of sheep. Those woolly, white imposters were grazing the hills at the west end of our lake and thirstily drinking our water. Oh, in retrospect, I had noticed a few steel fenceposts sticking up out of the ice when we had first strolled the borders with Mr. Harb. He mentioned them, casually, but I wasn't paying attention. After the thaw they were maybe fifteen feet from the west shoreline. That, we learned upon inquiry, was where our lake ended. From there on it was Ira Tobias's lake; which meant that Ira's lambs, rams and ewes had every right in the world to dip their snouts into the cool, clear depths.

Alice had learned that they and we, in fact, enjoyed riparian rights. Which means that anyone owning land adjacent to a body of water has full use of all the water. Not just for sheep but for fishing, swimming, water skiing, aquaplaning, snorkeling, baptizing, irrigating, any purpose that might occur. Once I learned about that fateful fifteen feet of unowned water I began to have visions. A phantom trailer court arose on the hills and hundreds of summer inhabitants crowded the narrow strip of beach, radios blaring, laughter and raucous song arising from the campfires that burned all night. Powerful speedboats caromed past our lakefront and waves washed away the sand we had put there for the amusement of our grandchildren. In my somewhat fevered imagination we became neighbors to a new Coney Island.

With less than sixty days of ownership behind us it became apparent to me that we had less land than we needed. Ninety acres was not enough. Alice tried to calm me, saying it probably didn't matter, but, if that were the case, why had she identified the problem, by name?

ALICE:

Somehow, in my mind, everything that was right was ours, anything that was wrong was mine. After all, I had found this place and, in every way possible, had urged its acquisition. One of the things Ken wanted most was a sense of isolation, privacy. That's what I thought we had bought from Mr. Harb. There were nights when I was wakeful and wondering if we had been deliberately deceived, if we simply hadn't asked enough questions. Maybe I had depended too much on my husband to do the business part of things. But now I wanted him to enjoy it, not fret about it. He never does fret long, not if there's something to be done. One day we walked Ira Tobias's acres. Shortly thereafter we visited his home.

KEN:

The land at the far end of the lake had been in the Tobias family for almost a hundred years. It is hilly, parklike, as meadows grazed by sheep are wont to be. A magnificent woods covers some eighteen acres of the sixty that comprise the parcel. There is a stone basement where a homestead house had been. Adjacent is an old dooryard with mulberry and walnut trees that a long-ago householder had planted and enjoyed. An ancient iron pump testifies to the one-time presence of water. The only building still standing is a fine barn, weathered gray, still in plumb with no sag in the sheet metal roof. The layout is attractive enough in its own right. Looking down and across a lovely twenty-acre lake, it is downright irresistible.

Ira Tobias' fondness for the place, however, had nothing to do with esthetics and everything to do with tradition. It had been the "home place" where some seventy years before he had been a boy. He and his brothers had trapped the marshland and hunted deer in the woods. This information all developed during the fairly regular visits we began to make to the neat little house where Ira, and his delightful wife, Louise, now lived. It was quite a distance away on a few acres that embraced an entire, landlocked ten acre lake. When we talked, Ira would sometimes mention how nice it was to have a lake that was all one's own.

I learned a lot about trapping muskrats and catching bull-heads during our time together. Alice exchanged recipes and sto-ries about children with Louise. We picked up local lore and some wonderful anecdotes about the schoolhouses of yore. Once Louise, who was in her eighties, amazed us by reciting an entire poem she had learned as a girl of ten. We enjoyed the old folks so much and liked them so much that I hated to bring up the subject of buying and selling. When I finally broached the possi-ble purchase of the desirable sixty acres, Ira's reply was com-pletely predictable. It had been in the family for two full genera-tions and it would stay in the family.

We continued to watch the sheep as the next couple of years passed. They would graze the hillside then come to the lake's edge to drink. They knew their riparian rights.

Long term thinking can induce a lot of headaches. If we took it a day at a time everything was marvelous. On a still, golden evening, in a boat drifting before the tiniest of breezes, with never another soul in sight, you could be the only person in the world. With a feisty half-pound bluegill on a wet fly and the tip of the rod flexing against it how could you possibly worry about the future of your real estate? It was ridiculous but some internal business voice would say:

"What about later? After Ira and Louise. . . ."

You could lose your concentration and maybe the fish, too.

There was a way to eliminate the riparian rights question. We had done it before, in order to improve the shoreline, and we could do it again. Lower the lake.

Remove its western edge from the neighboring land, bring it back onto our property. It could be done in the late summer after the sheep had been removed to another pasture so they wouldn't be denied water. It would be early enough in the fall for the amphibious inhabitants to adapt to a new shoreline and to hiber-nate safely. A new shoreline just might have an effect on negotia-tions.

So, once again we pulled a few boards and there was a mar-gin of mud around the water. The fenceposts that had been partially submerged stood on more-or-less dry land now, clearly defining the property line. The lake was all ours. Somewhat smaller, true enough, but completely landlocked by our acreage. The change in dimensions was never discussed with anyone. Our periodic visits with Ira and Louise continued as did reminiscing about times and events long past.

One evening, quite abruptly, Ira said, softly,

"If I was to sell you the sixty I'd want to keep grazing my sheep there as long as I live."

"That would be O.K. with me," I agreed.

"And there shouldn't be any trees cut from the woods," he added.

I nodded.

"The place means a lot to me and always has," Ira explained, "I'd like to see that it's taken proper care of."

"It will be."

"It would have to be on a land contract, with so much a year, so as I wouldn't get too much at a time," the canny old farmer continued, "and so I wouldn't be taxed so much."

That was certainly agreeable.

Only then did we talk price, which was quite reasonable.

Over the next few weeks, the deal was done and our original ninety acre farm became one hundred and fifty-three acres. Ira and Louise were our good friends and, once, before his eyesight dimmed, Ira rode with me in our Jeep truck to the top of the highest hill to have a final look around. He seemed satisfied.

We raised the lake, even increasing the height of the spillway so the water covered a greater area than before. For a good number of years the sheep continued to graze the grass and come down to the water's edge to quench their thirst. Their woolly whiteness against the green hillside enhanced the beauty of the scene.

It wasn't long after our second land acquisition that we decided to have the whole place surveyed. Nobody could remember when that had last been done. Old, decrepit, rusted barbed wire wandered to convenient trees, disappeared into

more or less impenetrable swamps. Finding and establishing the
real outlines of the property would tax the ingenuity and
endurance of the most professional of surveyors.

That's what William Hume Rogers proved to be. Well over
sixty, tough as oak, and thoroughly familiar with this part of the
country, he walked every foot of our perimeters. At the end of
three days he had covered fifty-nine miles and we knew exactly
where our line fences belonged. Alice was captivated by the
blueprints Mr. Rogers prepared. She looked at them carefully
and read the descriptions studiously.

"It's not the same," she puzzled.

"What's not the same?" I was a little impatient.

"This description and the one on the abstract."

She went to her files and pulled that document and examined it.

"Not the same," she repeated.

"You're just not reading it right," I pontificated. "The
lawyers know what they're doing. You're unduly worried."

"I'm going to show them the blueprint, anyway."

ALICE:

Ken tends to think me hysterical when I'm merely legitimately
concerned. The truth is that he's far more trusting than I am. He
believes that professionals make few mistakes. I know that they,
the doctors, lawyers, surveyors, bankers, are as much prone to
error as anyone. It embarrasses him to question their professional judgment and recommendations. It doesn't bother me.

KEN:

Alice simply showed them the survey and the title. They were
embarrassed. They had inadvertently neglected to include part of
the description. The land they had overlooked was the ten-acre

site of the dam that created the lake. The oversight was duly and fortunately corrected. Sometimes it pays to listen to an "unduly worried" wife.

ALICE:

To know that the lake, the whole lake, and everything around the lake, was truly ours brought me a kind of happiness that was almost unendurable. For the first time since I had boarded the train for my St. Louis wedding among strangers, I felt absolutely and completely at home. All I really wanted now was for Ken to feel the same way.

KEN:

To really enjoy a lake the size of ours, one obviously needs a boat. Shoreline angling isn't unproductive, but to find the Big Ones, you have to probe the deep spots beyond the reach of the longest cast. Our neighbor, Ken Granata, loaned us a big, old, red rowboat that had been stored in his barn. It filled the bill, temporarily, but we really needed a boat of our own. I made this point to Alice a number of times and really intended to do something about it. But, these were busy times at the office, and first things had to come first.

Nearly a year went by, summer passed, and we were into glorious October, the month of my birth. On the birthday weekend we drove up from the Detroit, parked the car, and walked down to the water's edge. There, incredibly, floating by the bank and tied to a tree, was a brand new, shiny twelve-foot long fibreglass rowboat!

"Happy birthday," said Alice.

"Unbelievable," said I.

She had driven up one day, picked up a little trailer we had, sped back to the city, gone to Sears Roebuck, bought the boat, had it loaded on the trailer, which she then concealed in a neighbor's garage. The following day, while I was at work, she hauled the whole shebang up to the lake, and, with another neighbor's help, wrestled the boat into the water and hitched it to a handy branch. That's all there was to it.

Over the years we've patched the fibreglass half a dozen times, to stop leaks. We've put on new oarlocks, repaired seats, kept it floating and useful. How many hundreds of fish have been hauled in, I can't say, and I know there have been some four and five pounders in the lot. That boat still makes me feel at home on the lake that Alice helped make all ours.

4

Someplace to Stay

ALICE:

WHEN THE LAKE first became ours, the land around it was practically houseless and that was fine with both of us. There was a shack in a grove of saplings along an old fence row. It had been built there by the two fishing enthusiasts from Chicago who had conceived the idea of placing a lake in the valley. After they had achieved that goal they needed a place to keep a boat and a few supplies. Thus the lumber and plywood shack. The floor was a few pieces of ridged tin lying on the ground. There was one small window and a narrow door. A basic structure for a boat but never intended for human habitation.

That's not how Ken saw it. He pointed out that there was a shelf just large enough for our Coleman camping stove. There was room for two narrow cots and a small folding table. Actually what we had, he said, was a nice, little cabin with everything we needed for rough, but adequate, living.

So, one raw day in March, just a few days after we became lake and landowners, we arrived at our new holdings carrying equipment plus provender from a nearby store. Ken, the practical man, managed, by walking sideways, to carry me, the sentimentalist, over the threshold. I glanced ahead and saw three mice scurry out from under the makeshift floor. I didn't mention it as I don't like to be petty when he's enjoying himself. After setting things up we took a brisk walk around the waterfront, just long enough to work up an appetite and get thoroughly chilled. It was fairly windy and we discovered upon returning to our cozy, little cabin that it was far from windproof.

With all the enthusiasm of the real outdoorsman, Ken pumped up the pressure in our camp stove and lit it.

"That will warm things up," he promised.

I put our hamburger patties in the skillet and placed it on the stove which promptly started to slide down the wobbly shelf that held it. Ken found a board and braced it. I put my gloves back on and kept them on while I waited for the beans to warm. It got very smoky as I flipped the hamburgers so Ken opened the window, and it fell out of its frame. We sat on two camp stools, paper plates on our knees, and ate.

"Isn't this great," he said, four or five times.

Before we left he got the window back in, tightened the door hinges and fixed a hasp and lock on the door to discourage intruders. (I still hadn't mentioned the mice.) Fortunately he hadn't set up our cots. We loaded them, plus the stove and table, back into the station wagon. There didn't seem to be any need for talk. There was a definite need for someplace to stay, and we found a vacancy at the local motel.

Through the peculiar providence that was operating in our behalf in those days, our nearest neighbors, the Granatas, took a real interest in our activities. They had been through it all themselves. He had been a police officer and she a school teacher in a Detroit suburb, and they had already decided to spend the rest of their lives as rural residents. With a huge investment of thought, toil and tenacity, they had converted a ramshackle farm house into a lovely home that overlooked our property.

Their house and barn had, in fact, been part of the original farm that was now our land and lake. We stopped by often on our weekends to visit and consult. They knew about our change in viewpoint concerning roughing it in the shack.

We were back in the city when Ken Granata called one evening. He had found a mobile home for sale and thought it might provide us with temporary quarters. It was ten years old, ten feet wide and fifty feet long and all ours for $1,000. We said we'd take it sight unseen. He, bless him, said he would make arrangements to have it moved, set up and leveled for a modest sum.

"Great!" we thought. "Our housing problems are solved."

It was all in place when we made our Saturday run to the property shortly thereafter. I wouldn't want to be thought of as a female chauvinist; but I have come to the reluctant conclusion that most men don't have the same aversion to dirt that most women do. This mobile home had been the bachelor quarters for two deputies from the sheriff's department and I'm sure they had been comfortable and happy. There was dust, untouched, everywhere. There were cobwebs where generations of spiders lived, caught flying insects, reproduced and died without disturbance. The windows were opaque, the walls filmed over with a sort of greasy glaze. None of this is by the way of complaint. The portable dwelling was a rare bargain. The refrigerator and range were crusty, but worked, as did all the plumbing. An oil furnace checked out fine. But a little work would be required to make it habitable from my point of view.

We didn't stay overnight.

A wonderful cleaning lady had helped me for years in the city and I invited her to spend a couple of days at our new country place to help put things in order. We had a lovely drive up, stopping for a good lunch in town. She admired the view as we came down the lane and saw the lake framed by the two maple trees. We parked and strolled to the red and white metal edifice propped up on concrete blocks. I opened the door and we stepped inside.

"My God," Catherine said, "Let's go home!"

All we tried to do the first day was make the place fit to sleep in without wondering what little creatures might still be inhabiting it. By the end of two days it was decent and we were both worn out. It was late afternoon and we would need to start for Detroit within the hour. Now, though, we sat on the seat-sprung sofa and looked through clean windows framed by some old beige curtains I had brought along. The lake sparkled and it had warmed up considerably.

"This will be real nice," Catherine smiled.

It certainly beat the shack in the hollow.

There were still a few details to be handled for really gracious living, like installing a well, pump and septic system. There was the also the matter of a mad thermostat that wouldn't allow the furnace to shut off so we had to open the windows when the heat was on. But, all in all, the place was livable. At first, that is.

Then, inevitably, our weekend place in the country became an entertainment center. Buck, my husband's brother, is his twin so they like to have shared birthday parties.

When fall colored its way into the year and the annual celebration was planned, it seemed so logical to have it at the lake. The air would be like wine, the leaves magnificent. We could barbecue, and it would be an event. Rain, obviously, could change all that; and, sure enough, after everybody had arrived, it rained. In the mobile home, all at one time, were the two of us and our two teenagers, Buck, his wife, Nita, and their three big boys, young Buck, Mike, and Tim, and, finally, my mother-in-law. Ten people and a dog is a houseful in a living-dining area planned for just four. So we had a buffet that spilled over into the bedrooms, bathroom and out the front door when the downpour slowed to a drizzle. Everybody had fun, and the two little maple saplings that were Buck's birthday present to Ken got off to a nice moist start.

But when the party did break up and our eight guests were leaving, Mom Jones said an obvious truth.

"One of these days you're going to need a bigger place."

Again, the Granatas were the catalyst who brought about

change. May had saved us a newspaper story from the local gazette and gave it to us one weekend. The headline was: SPACE WORKS OVERTIME IN HIS HOUSES. There were pictures of attractive, unusual houses and a story that said, in part:

"Each of these houses was completely enclosed in one day after a pre-built core containing plumbing, wiring, heating and cabinets was set in place on the foundation."

Sounded interesting. Elsewhere in the story it explained that the builder, one Gerald Davidson of Union City, Michigan, was a consistent innovater in his field.

He had built houses in the dead of winter under the protection of an inflated plastic tent that would hold heat. He had turned an old quarry that had been a community liability into a lovely lagoon and had built low-rent apartments around it. Union City is sixty miles from the lake, but Ken put down the paper and said:

"Let's go see him."

"Now?"

"Sure."

"Without calling?"

"It's a nice day for a ride."

It was and we did and, later, we would refer to Jerry as "the poor man's Frank Lloyd Wright."

There are no blueprints for our home. The building took form from exchanged conversations between us and Jerry. At first he was loath to tackle a job so far from his base. But my persuasive husband described the lake and the land. That did the trick. It was a marvelous day when Jerry showed up and he loved what he saw.

"The house will just be a pimple," he said. "It will hardly break the view."

We had said we just wanted a small place for weekends and vacations but his description was almost too apt.

"But, when people get inside," he continued, "Wow! We'll have big windows facing south looking out on the lake, and they'll get a sense of space and wonder and they'll be amazed."

"Sounds good," said Ken, who loves the dramatic.

Jerry interviewed us like a talk show host. What did we like to do? How would we spend our days when it rained?

Did I like to cook? Did Ken like to read? Did we have any hobbies like painting or collecting stamps? Were we savers or thrower-outers? What colors did we like? How much would we be entertaining? He listened a lot and came back with sketches and lists, and a basic philosophy.

"We'll use the least expensive materials," he explained, "like plastic pipe and magnetic door latches instead of the usual inset kind."

He would use all the money-saving methods and synthetic materials that have developed in the mobile home business, which is where Jerry learned his trade. When you think about the beautiful interiors that are now taken for granted in this kind of alternative housing and how comparatively little it costs, it is something of a wonder.

However, Jerry wasn't just saving so we could put the money into stocks and bonds.

"What we save by cutting some corners," he announced, "we'll spend on the good life."

That's how we came to have one of the very first microwave ovens, an Amana. Though the thought of this new-fangled invention cooking our food with *rays* secretly terrified me, I knew better than to object. Not with two forceful men to scoff at imaginary fears.

"It'll save you cooking time," Jerry said firmly. "You're not coming here to spend your weekends in the kitchen, and," he told Ken, "we'll put a steam sauna in the bathroom for you. I imagine you'll do a lot of strenuous stuff and that'll keep you from going back to the office all stove up on Monday mornings."

There was a Murphy bed in the dining room, too, the kind that folds up into a wall, and that I'd only seen before in filmed comedy skits.

"For guests," was the explanation. "You seem to be pretty gregarious and you'll be having considerable company. Just wheel the dining table aside, drop the bed and you have a guest room without adding floorspace."

I saw our idyllic, alone-together life disappearing.

Jerry liked to philosophize. He said that a man, his wife and their house should be a happy triangle. He talked about the way primitive peoples shared the planning and building of their shelters, the sod huts and log cabins of our immediate forefathers. He never drew plans, but he and Ken, with words, constructed castles in the air.

Meanwhile, in Jerry's factory in Union City, what he called our "core house" took shape. The front hall, bathroom, and kitchen, with all plumbing and electrical connections, was the core. It was complete. The wallpaper I had chosen was on, floor covering down, and appliances installed, including the microwave and steam sauna as well as dishwasher, stove and refrigerator. When it was finished, it was a thirty-two foot long, ten foot wide box, wrapped in plastic.

While it was being put together, another man we had met was doing the on-site work. Ed McPharlin has long been one of the most respected and successful builders in Barry County. His houses are solid values. Everything fits right, works right, looks right. He thinks carefully, speaks slowly and likes exact and clear understandings.

He had been recommended to us as the most reliable and honest of contractors and had proven to be just that when he installed our septic tank, drain field and hooked them up to the mobile home. Ed is tall, and strong with clear blue eyes under shaggy, reddish brows. Sometimes you're not exactly sure what he's thinking. Like when we told him about Jerry and the core house and how we wanted him to help.

Because Ed had become a friend as well as a contractor, he agreed to ride over to Union City with me and to talk with Jerry. He was inclined to be a little wary of my ideas about housing since I had once suggested that we might enclose our mobile home in an A-frame. He explained that such a structure would have to be ninety feet tall to be proportionate and he doubted if I wanted a small skyscraper by the lake. On the drive to Jerry's he indicated some doubts about the wisdom of the core idea but said he was willing to listen.

If ever two men in the same business were complete contradictions as personalities, those men were Ed and Jerry. Where Ed was taciturn, Jerry was a fountain of ideas, thoughts, information and questions. Everytime Jerry mentioned a new material or method Ed made probing inquiry as to proof of performance. But gradually, they arrived at an understanding and Ed agreed to supervise the necessary excavating, build the foundation and ready it for the arrival of the core. The hole in the ground was duly dug, the concrete blocks went up into walls and after hitches, glitches and delays, it was time for the core to be delivered.

One concern was the changeable Michigan weather. We had all agreed that the Big Event must occur on a dry day. The weekend picked was forecast as sunny and pleasant and that Saturday morning Jerry got off to an early start. Nothing the height and length of our package had ever been hauled over the narrow, winding gravel roads that lead to the lake. On the way Jerry and his assistants, Harold and Paul, had to stop and saw off a lot of low hanging tree limbs before the awkward rig could get through. Then it began to rain.

When the rain began, Ken and I were sure the project was canceled for another week. We disappointedly dressed in rain gear and rowed across the lake to look for mushrooms. Before disappearing into the woods, we glanced back at the house site and saw a big truck pulling a bigger trailer on which sat the huge black plastic-wrapped core. The caravan made a wide turn into our drive. We ran to the boat and rowed back across at a frantic rate. It was raining hard and the clay around the completed foundation was getting slick as only clay can. By the time the behemoth caravan had manuevered its way down the driveway and backed up to the carrying walls, I was a certified wreck. Ken stayed outside to help. I hid in the mobile home, pulled the curtains and turned the radio up full volume. I wanted to drown out the sound of what I felt would be the inevitable crash of the core into the basement hole.

Later, hours later, centuries later, I heard the door open and close. It was Ken.

"It fell in, didn't it?" I asked.

"Damn near," my husband said.

I found out later that he wasn't exaggerating. As the core was levered off the flatbed truck that carried it and onto the bearing walls that Ed McPharlin had built, it started to slide sideways. Only the desperately applied strength of Jerry, Paul, Harold and finally, Ken, had prevented a disaster. I'm glad I hid.

From that day forward things went well. All the prefabricated units came over as scheduled and were incorporated into a house. A stone chimney climbed skyward in back. Some beautiful Indiana cut stone adorned the front. We added a redwood deck to the upper story and a patio below. The patio was poured concrete, but Ed not only gave it a freeform design but devised a pattern that made it look like flagstone. Like Jerry's, his was a creative touch.

Much of the work was done while we were back in the city and we only checked it on weekends. But I did manage to occasionally manufacture a good reason to drive the 125 miles in the middle of the week. Construction was a sight to behold. Jerry, in his sixties, did everything at the dead run. He was immensely powerful and would tote and carry heavy beams single handedly while issuing a steady stream of instructions to his assistants. Paul, lean, swarthy, part-Indian, was utterly silent, always intent on a single operation whether it was driving nails or cutting patterns with a power saw. Harold, bespectacled, older, acted as a sort of go-between, relaying instructions from Jerry to Paul, who would simply nod and go on with what he was doing. None of them paid much attention to me and I was happy just to wander around the acreage, listening to the music of power tools and hammers singing of our house. Within weeks it was ready for occupancy.

As with all things unorthodox, there were a few problems.

We had installed some motel-size heating and air-conditioning units, and there was a lot of trouble in making them fit properly. The first weekend that my mother-in-law came to stay in the new house it rained hard during the night. In the morning she called to me.

"Alice, the lake has risen."

"What?"

"There's a pool of water by my bed. We must be in the middle of a flood."

We had to recaulk around the air conditioner.

If one of us was watching TV and the other taking a steam bath, the circuit breaker would kick out and, suddenly, neither of us would be doing either. Some rewiring was in order. And the shower door opened the wrong way. But we were under roof. The view was magnificent, as Jerry had envisioned. Our weekend retreat was complete. Living room, dining-guest room, bedroom, bath and kitchen upstairs; a tiny laundry room, storage room, office for Ken and family room downstairs.

Everything we would ever need, I thought.

Ken seemed pleased, too.

KEN:

I was. This tiny house, this bucolic retreat, was the perfect haven. Weekends that had once been given over to cocktail parties with colleagues and clients could now be salvaged. It was simple to say, "Sorry, we'll be out of town."

There was the bonus benefit of not having to repay invitations with large parties given expressly for that purpose. Let the sterling silver tarnish, the fine china gather dust, the liquor supply remain undiminished

There was, admittedly, a twinge when the Executive V.P. indicated that you had been missed at the client's fiftieth anniversary soiree, a moment of insecurity when it was pointed out that the great man himself had inquired about your absence. To counter that was the incomparable feeling of *escape*. That, and the new Alice, who, like a diminutive and feminine Antaeus, took strength from the earth that was now ours and the house that more than sheltered us.

Double Living, Double Fun

KEN:

SOMETIMES, fortune is kinder to us than we deserve. When Alice's random telephone call to WTAK led us to the lake, we thought our futures involved continued residence in the Detroit area. But, my company decided that Chicago was the place for me. Luckily, our new country place was just about halfway between the Windy City and the Motor City and all the move did was add an hour to travel time.

ALICE:

The fabric of our lives was being rewoven by the fates that brought us to the country. Once, all initiatives were Ken's. His erratic hours shaped our rising and retiring and the times when we, as a family, ate together. His needs were ours, whether it was getting him packed and delivered to the airport for a protracted production trip to Hollywood, or planning a cocktail do for two dozen friends and associates. Now I had my own priorities for about sixty hours of every week, starting Fridays at 5:00 P.M.and ending Monday mornings. If it took cajoling, I could cajole; pouting, when necessary; a bit of temper as a last resort. Whatever was required to move us out beyond the city limits when the working week was over, that, I was prepared to do. At first there was occasional resistance, but, before long we were scheduled like a railroad.

KEN:

Item: Finish all business by 4:45 P.M., Fridays. Alice was waiting at the building entrance to pick me up. We were on our way, ahead of the 5:00 o'clock Freeway Frolic. With a little luck we could lead the pack across the city limits.

Item: Bring along a Mason Jar martini. Pull off at a roadside park for an abbreviated cocktail hour.

Item: Formulate finger-food dinners. Chicken legs, pickles and potato chips can be munched while on the move. No restaurants, no rest stops, just get there.

Now find the two flaming maple trees at the top of the hill with your headlights. Drift down the long driveway to a stop, Get out into the velvet night and seek the Big Dipper and the Queen's Chair in the sky. Breathe. Out goes the city air, in comes the country. Then, to the faucet in the kitchen and draw a draught of water from the well. Cold and pure, no chlorine, fluoride, iron, sulphur, mineral, just a crystal liquid from its subterranean grotto deep beneath us. Out on the balcony for a look at the shimmering silver of the lake. Then to bed and to sleep in the wonderful silence.

No alarm clock is needed at the lake. Our projects for each weekend had us up at dawn. They had all been set down in a thin, blue folder entitled Soil and Water Conservation Plan. That had been put together by John Hamp, county Soil Conservationist, at our request. He had walked the acres with us, probed our ultimate aims and responded with The Folder. Two areas were designated as Wildlife and Recreation Land and the directives for Field 1 stipulated:

> Twenty-six acres will be kept open for wildlife by mowing to control brush and keep vegetation green.
>
> One acre of raw and eroding area will be seeded to rye grass and Chewing's Fescue.

There was an agenda for Field 2, as well:

> Two acres of exposed open slopes to be planted to White and Austrian pines. Spaced 8′ in rows 8′ apart. (See Job Sheet 622.)
>
> Wildlife habitat development 1 acre. Food plots will be planted on the contour in strips 20′ by 30′ in length. Plants may include corn, wheat, sorghum, soybean or buckwheat.
>
> Two acres of assorted food producing shrubs will be planted in clumps for wildlife food and cover. (See Job Sheets 810, 812, 813.)
>
> Fish Pond Management. Algae and excessive weed growth will be controlled by chemical and mechanical means. Regulate harvest so about 10–14 bluegills are removed for each bass caught. Undersized bluegills will not be returned to pond. Encourage year around use by ice fishing.

With an agenda like that, is it any wonder that we got up with the sun? That we stayed up late reading bulletins, pamphlets and Job Sheets?

Best part of the plan was the fish harvesting with a fly rod in late spring. When a big bluegill hit a tiny, floating rubber spider and started his circling fight, that was Conservation at its best!

While the Land Plan was good for hours of earnest endeavor, it never quite occupied the entire weekend. There was always time and need for exploration, and, oh, the things that we discovered.

There is a marsh at the far end of the lake, two acres of tangled underbrush, willow saplings, spongy ground and muck that can swallow you up to your knees. In it we found blackberry bushes that grew the biggest berries that we had ever seen. They were sweet and a couple of dozen would fill a quart box. Then there was watercress, fifty square feet of the peppery leaves that gave salads and sandwiches a flair of flavor. In the fall we found wild apple trees. One bore a yellow fruit that was tart and tangy, another a dappled red for applesauce and apple butter, a third had picture book beauties unblemished and flavorful for the table bowl. Sometimes we would startle deer, watch their bobbing white flags as they fled, coughing warnings to everything in the woods. There were potholes in the woods from which mallards might be flushed and morel mushrooms hiding under leaves and giant white puffballs in the clearings. Our fence lines were, indeed, the borders of a magic kingdom which abounded in hidden treasures.

A weekend of working and walking taught us to appreciate some of the ideas in the house that Jerry built. To ease aching muscles in the steambath was sheer delight. Nothing fancy about it, just a box two feet by one foot set in the bathroom wall, with pipes leading to the shower head. You climbed in the shower stall after setting the dial for twelve or fifteen minutes and within minutes, steam came rolling out of the faucet. Just as you were about to yell for help, the steam clicked off and, then, following instructions reluctantly, you turned on the cold shower. When it was all over you understood how Finns must feel after a sauna and a roll in the snow. Glowing, healthy and a model of hardihood.

That's the way it was on Sunday night as weekends rolled to a close. On Monday mornings, while it was still dark, our headlights would pick up the two big maples that stood guard at the top of the driveway. We'd wave goodbye to them and settle in for the long drive back to the city. There was a thermos of coffee for the road and, generally, not a lot of conversation. Each of us was savoring recollections. We would pick up morning news and music on the car radio and watch the sun come up as we hit the expressways. As we pulled to a stop outside the building where I worked there would be a brief exchange:

"Before next Friday pick us up some work gloves."

"O.K. Should we invite anybody up next weekend?"

"Maybe for Sunday. Let's keep Saturday for working around the place."

"It was nice, wasn't it?"

"Gorgeous."

"Bye, honey."

"Bye."

Then she would be off to our very nice apartment and I'd zoom skyward on the express elevator to my very nice office, and our hearts were still somewhere just south of the two maple trees. I suppose we still appeared fairly normal to our friends and associates. At dinner parties we might pull out pictures of the land and the lake when others would rather talk about a Mediterranean vacation. At business conferences there were times when the matter at hand got lost in recollection of the reel singing as a whopper bass headed for the bottom.

"Well, what do you think, Jones?" someone would ask concerning whatever was under discussion.

"Sounds good, uh, but would you run through it one more time? I missed some of the subtleties in the presentation."

Sharing the place with friends became a preoccupation with me. I was always thinking about who to invite.

ALICE:

Knowing Ken's gregarious nature, that was to be expected. When he had first declared that he wanted a retreat, a place to be alone by ourselves, he was hurting. It wasn't in his nature not to share. Actually, I'm something of a loner and would have been quite content to remain as undiscovered as Robinson Crusoe. But that simply wasn't to be.

KEN:

Among the earliest of invited parties was my secretary, Jean, a lovely, loyal and unmistakably English lady. In speech she was something of a Julie Andrews, in appearance, Deborah Kerr and in skills of her office, simply incomparable. She helped with letters and documents relating to the transactions that made us lake owners and, naturally, at some point I suggested that she might like to see the place.

A mutually agreeable weekend was determined, and she accompanied us on our drive up to spend Saturday night and Sunday. By prearrangement, a young man she had been seeing was to come up Sunday morning so the two of them would have time together in an idyllic setting.

He arrived on schedule, quite early, despite a heavy downpour during most of the night and showers in the morning. It was gray and misty and probably reminded Jean of the moors. Actually we could hear the baying of hounds in the distance. Undeterred by the less than favorable conditions, our doughty Briton borrowed a pair of Alice's oversize boots and she and her companion strode off toward the distant pasture. In twenty minutes they were back with Jean in a state of considerable agitation. When she leaped lightly over a small boulder, she landed with her feet just inches away from a coiled serpent. If ours was an Eden, she was no Eve, and reptiles held no fascination for her. As the startled snake reacted by wrapping itself around her ankle Jean gave a ladylike scream and leapt into the arms of the unperturbed man alongside.

"It was only a garter snake," he later said, "and not very big."

We believe it marked a turning point in their relationship and they have now been married for a number of years.

Any country place will have its share of snakes, and they are excellent conversation starters. When a party embarks on a walk, it's a great idea to point out places where reptilian adventures have taken place. Everyone gets into single file and nobody contests for the lead.

Another early visitor had an experience quite the opposite of Jean's.

Tom Lowe was a close friend of our son's and in his second year of medical school. When he made his first visit he brought along a girl who was obviously smitten. Admiration shone in her eyes, affection in the way she clung to his arm. He liked it, too, for the first part of the afternoon. Then, for some reason beyond recall, I saw a large blacksnake in the dock area and smote it with a shovel. Normally I wouldn't have bothered it but I suppose that it seemed necessary to dispatch it so that guests wouldn't be alarmed. Anyway I called Tom and he came to look at the rather large remains. Now his eyes shone.

"I've always wanted to articulate one," he exclaimed. "Can I have it?"

As the afternoon wore on he skinned the creature, removed every vestige of its flesh, reduced it to a complete and impressive skeleton, carefully mounted on a board. His date feigned a sort of horrified interest for about fifteen minutes and then it was too much for her. She spent a lot of time in the kitchen talking to Alice. I don't believe the young couple ever had another outing in the country, or in the city for that matter.

Maybe there's an overemphasis on reptilian reminisences but there was one with somewhat serious overtones. Eddie Birnbryer, and his wife, Dorothy, were our guests. Their early spring visits have become an annual event. Long an avid golfer, and no fisherman at all, Eddie still manages, somehow, to catch at least one monster bass per year. Twice it's been the record for the season. He takes his good fortune with aplomb and never seems surprised at the fact that his record is better than that of many far more devoted anglers. One year he was spared an experience that might have startled even him.

It was a windy day and therefore not great for floating the lake. So we decided to work from the shoreline and had been doing so. On arrival at the dam Eddie lingered to make a few casts and I started across the earthen embankment. Suddenly, about five feet in front of me in the high grass that edged the mown pathway, something moved. I stopped, looked hard and saw the S-curve flat against the ground. The skin was lighter than that of the familiar, harmless water moccasin, the raised head seemed more triangular.

Tentatively I poked the creature with the end of the slender flyrod in my hand. It straightened out and glided deeper into the grass and down the dam face towards some logs. Before it disappeared I saw its tail, a tiny sort of honeycomb of horn that rustled as the snake moved. It was a rattler, a massasauga rattler, the state's only poisonous reptile. Eddie called to me:

"Nothing's happening here." He swished his rod in a casting motion. "Maybe I should come out there."

"It's no good here, either. Why don't we head for the house."

We did, and since nobody else would be in the vicinity of the dam for the rest of their visit, nothing was said about the unexpected intruder. Ed and Dorothy went home and to this day I've never mentioned the episode, although it gives me shudders to think of what might have happened if he had preceded me across the impoundment.

Business took me away from our place the next morning and, indeed for the week. On the day we returned I put on high leather boots, took a 20 gauge shotgun and started a forty-five minute patrol of he dam. That's how long it took before I caught the glint of something in a wide crack between two rocks.

One shot did it and I extricated the still striking body from its hiding place with a long stick. It thrashed and struck and struck again at the empty air and then it was still. There were seven segments to the rattle. Never once had it sounded its famed alarm. Two days later, upon hearing about the episode, neighbor Charlie Tobias pronounced some disquieting words.

"They always go in pairs. What you should have done is covered the dead one with an old tarp or blanket. Later t'other one will crawl in beside it and you could get it, too. That way you wouldn't have to worry."

Since I'd flung the remains into an inaccessible place I couldn't follow the formula. So, for a while, I worried.

Visitors. With them it was double adventure, double fun.

Perhaps no guest ever showed more hardihood or panache than Will Cowan, from Hollywood. A friend and colleague of many years' standing, he had a zest for living unequalled in my experience. On my business visits to the West Coast, he turned weekends into enthralling escapades.

There was the time that we ran a leaking boat from Newport Beach to Catalina Island with me manning the pumps all the way. We just made a small repair marina before my arm gave out. While a mechanic hunted for the problem, Will cracked out champagne and cold fowl and, feet awash, we had our swanky lunch. Later we had to be towed 27 miles back to the mainland on a very long towrope. Nearing shore we cut through a sailing regatta. If cuss words had been naval salvos we'd have been blown out of the water.

Another time he inveigled me into taking one of those package trips from Los Angeles to Las Vegas. Aboard an ancient four-engine plane we lumbered through the night and listened to an equally ancient comedian do routines and play a midget piano while overage bunnies served domestic champagne to a raucous crowd of gamblers.

That's the stuff of which memories are made. Whenever Will shows up there's likely to be adventure ahead.

It was a blustery, snowy Friday evening when he came to visit us in our apartment. He was enroute from Hollywood to New York on a business trip and had the weekend to spare. Our plan was to stay off the streets and out of the raw, cutting wind so we had made dinner reservations at a fine French restaurant that could be reached without leaving the building. A quiet meal, a good visit, maybe some time at the Art Institute the next day, that was the agenda. But Will arrived early, the talk, inevitably, got around to the lake and, as we enthused, he listened intently. Then, rather abruptly, he said:

"Let's go see it."

"Will," I explained, "It's nearly two hundred miles from here."

I had already opted for a weekend at home, because of Will's visit. Alice had agreed. To my surprise, she entered the conversation.

"We wouldn't want to tire you, but it's not really a bad drive. You could sleep on the way."

He shrugged.

"So, I've traveled eight hundred today, what's a couple hundred more?"

"It takes about three hours to get there," Alice chimed in, "it's seven-thirty already and our dinner reservations are for eight o'clock."

I looked at her. Her words were one thing but she had the lake look in her eyes.

Will, ever the man of action, had already picked up his magnificent camel hair topcoat and was putting it on. Alice got her fun fur from the closet while I was calling the restaurant to cancel. By seven forty-five we were at the gas pumps in the garage and at eight we were pulling on to the tollroad out of town. A few flakes of snow were drifting down.

By nine o'clock it was snowing hard and we were all ravenously hungry. There was an all-night truck stop just across the state line and I mentioned it.

"They say truckers know the best places to eat," Will volunteered.

We decided to give it a try and pulled in among a herd of semis, tankers, huge vans and flatbeds. Outside of the waitresses, Alice was the only woman on the premises and Will's camel hair coat was certainly unique. We found an inconspicuous table that moved us out of the mainstream and ordered. Apparently winter had come upon the proprietors as a surprise, and there was little or no heat. Cold drafts swept across the floor and iced our feet. The food was a little better than tepid, the pie leaden, the coffee bitterly strong. We ate silently and swiftly. On the way out Will remarked:

"Another legend lost."

"What?"

"Truckers and good food. Forget it."

By now the snow was sticking to the roads and I was grateful for my front-wheel drive vehicle and its ability to claw through the stuff. I knew that, if the blizzard continued, we'd have a reasonable chance to make it through the drifted backroads that led to our driveway.

It was midnight and still snowing as we traced tire tracks in the whiteness between the maples and pulled up to the house. Fortunately the thermostats had been set at fifty degrees and it didn't take long to get the place comfortable. We had drinks, Alice made sandwiches and a fire soon crackled in the Franklin stove. Will went out the back door onto the deck after I turned on the floodlights that illuminated the hillside and the edge of the lake. He came back in and said it all:

"Unbelievable. Absolutely unbelievable."

We only had half of the next day to share. The sun was brilliant and the lake had a film of ice over it. Cardinals flashed at the bird feeder and two deer ran across the hill. We watched it all from the windows over a breakfast of eggs, sausage, hot biscuits and fresh coffee.

"You should start a truck stop," Will suggested.

The snow was too deep for walking around in our city shoes and our winter gear hadn't yet been deployed. There was some rather complicated telephoning to be done to get Will on his way again. Somehow he arranged a flight out of the nearest small city and connections that would put him where he wanted to be when he needed to be there. Late in the morning we negotiated the driveway and backroads and found the highway ploughed and clear. The countryside glistened and Will remarked that he hadn't seen snow like this in a dozen years. When we said goodbye at the airport he put it simply:

"With a place like you've got and all it must mean to you, I don't see how you can go back to the city."

That refrain was repeated at other times by other people. We heard it when the still water reflected the blazing hills of autumn. It sounded at the end of a summer's day of fabulous fishing. It echoed in our minds when we knew we were going away for a long, long time. Business, suddenly moved us to Australia, half a world away. Somewhere along the line, maybe in a 747 high above the Pacific, we moved toward a decision. Maybe that should be *I* moved toward a decision. Alice's had been made long ago.

ALICE:

Isn't life together really a series of trade-offs? Young love had led me to the metropolitan merry-go-around and it was fun, if dizzying. But the yearning for space and seasonal beauty, for relatively simple relationships and a kind of country closeness, had remained with me. So, as these wonderful weekends worked their magic on us both, I hoped, and, in these years of later love, Ken knew what I wanted and gave it to me.

6

On Making a Very Major Move

KEN:

FIVE NEW CALENDARS had hung on the kitchen wall since the house that Jerry built was moved on to Ed McPharlin's firm foundation. Between long weekends and short vacations we averaged around a hundred and twenty days a year in that house. They were simply better than the days in our lovely, downtown city apartment. Not just because one was a base for the job that supported us, and the other our hideaway. It was more than that.

There's an indivisible quality to marital happiness. If each of us is really enjoying life, then both of us are truly happy. That state, poetically referred to as bliss, is impossible to enjoy alone, and rare enough for a couple. Without overstatement, we found days of pure enchantment at the Lake.

It started with Alice. The kind of highs that had sometimes come my way during exciting years in business were now coming to her. They had to do with the discovery that hummingbirds were drinking from the Coral Bells in the garden; that our grand-kids loved a day on the tiny beach we had built; that we could simply sit silently on a hillside with the wind making all the music we needed.

Those things, that brought her joy, were becoming my plea-sures, too. Why should we rush to them on Fridays, and flee them with Monday's dawn? That was one side of the question. Could we completely forsake a way of living that served us well for thirty years? That was the other. The answer was in something that had happened to Alice, something she hadn't told me about at the time. Here, in her words, is the story.

ALICE:

Shortly after buying the property I began to suffer from symptoms that convinced me I had a serious heart problem. After an electric cardiogram, and various tests, the doctor con-ducted a verbal examination. His questions, my answers:

Q: What have you been doing lately?

A: Oh, going to the country.

Q: Where is that?

A: It's ninety acres of beautiful, rolling hills, with a twenty-acre lake right in the middle of it and it's all ours!

Q: Do you know what's wrong with you?

A: *(Fearfully)* No, doctor, I don't.

He looked at me, his eyes crinkled and he grinned. "You're suffering from extreme happiness," he said.

I guess your heart can almost burst with joy.

KEN:

Alice simply wanted me to learn to share her kind of wealth.

Now, suddenly there was the opportunity to phase out of the known past and into an indistinct, but inviting, future. As a bridge, there was this unexpected assignment of work overseas for a couple of years. Then, the return and the clean break with urban life; the chance for more solitude and silence and less cultural and professional excitement; the tradeoff of a multiplicity of contacts and acquaintances for some close neighbors and more time with true friends; a transfer of allegiance from The Good of The Company to the improvement and shared enjoyment of Aurohn Lake. It had that name now, inspired by a question we had heard repeatedly on Monday mornings:

"Did you have a nice weekend?"

"Yep. Wonderful."

"Oh? Where were you?"

"At the lake."

"What lake?"

"Well ... uh ... we've got our own lake."

It always brought a surprised look and usually led to more conversation. So we decided to make it official. While the body of water showed on aerial photographs and county maps, it was untitled. So we invented a word.

Aurohn. Say it phonetically, with a long O. Awr-own. Our Own Lake.

You'll find it on the letterheads we had printed and, yes, it's on the county map now. A lot of people think it's an Indian name. Aurohn Lake we named it, and our one and only place to live it would become.

It wasn't an easy decision, particularly for me. Trading in the magic of Chicago's Michigan Avenue, the glamor of 747's, for a bumpy country road was a little spooky. We talked, or rather I talked and Alice listened. There *were* books to be written, fish to be caught, thoughts to be thought. After fairly interminable arguments with myself, the decision to cut all the old strings was made. It was mutual and irrefutable.

Alice glowed. Then, as she'll tell you, she got pretty busy. While I was half-a-world away, making ads for Australian, Malaysian, Singaporean, Hong Kong and Thai markets, Alice was softening the effects of our own, personal future shock. Here are her recollections.

ALICE:

Moving isn't all that big a thing to me. We've done it fairly frequently during Ken's peripatetic career. This time it was as simple as putting everything from a very large apartment into storage, saving out some linens, a few knick-knacks and my favorite cookbook. These would be part of my luggage when I joined my husband in the "fully furnished" house he'd found in Northbridge, Australia, a lovely suburb across the bay from Sydney.

Two things about this move were different and difficult. Leaving our beloved poodle, Robin, was something we had never done before. But Australia requires a long quarantine period before foreign dogs are allowed in the country so we asked Ken's brother and sister-in-law if they would dog-sit for two years and they kindly consented. Even so, we felt like heels at this desertion. The other big difference was leaving a place I really loved. That had never happened before because I'd never felt about any place we had lived like I felt about the lake. But the plans were made. Ken wrote out careful guidelines about visitation rights, care and maintenance, and then we contacted dear Jerry Davidson about building for our future. Ken and Jerry both have a marvelous way of oversimplifying.

"Just build a big box where we can put the stuff we've got in storage," was Ken's stated building plan. "And try to bring it in at not more that $20,000."

"I've got a pretty good idea of what you want," Jerry agreed.

He probably did have but I felt we needed something a little more specific. In his great, free-wheeling way Jerry did verbal sketches of a soaring balcony bedroom, a two-story high window wall overlooking the water, a sweeping open staircase. It sounded impressive, and I said I would like to see plans and blueprints. Jerry nodded. Before we left we agreed on general specifications about the size of joists, the type of insulation, wiring and such. A three-page document full of words like vapor barrier, tectum, Spandrel, thermopane, truss, mansard was drawn up and typed in triplicate by Ken.

That was it. No pictures, sketches or blueprints. We went to Australia believing that would all be forthcoming and that our dreams would swiftly be transformed into realities.

Four months later we got word that the foundation had been poured. Then, silence. Figuring that mail went both ways I summoned up an amateur architect's best skills and drew detailed plans, right down to where furniture would be placed. Off they went, by air, to Jerry. Outside of an imaginative crayon sketch of the way the exterior would look, which he sent us much later, no other drawings were ever made! Only faith, some supervision and reporting by Ken Granata, and Jerry's genius saved us from a fiasco. Later we heard the reasons. In his drive to bring imaginative housing to western Michigan, Jerry had overextended himself physically and had been ordered by his doctor to slow down. Our project was on temporary hold.

Whatever happened back there, I could take advantage of where I was to make the house, when it was finished, a reflection of our adventures in other lands. There were big, white, woolly sheepskin rugs from the stations of New South Wales. They would warm our feet in the balcony bedroom. In Singapore I found two graceful brass chandeliers shaped by Indian workmen. They could be suspended from six foot chains and would glow in the high window. I thought a lot about that window. With what does one cover a window that's eighteen feet wide and twelve feet high? In Singapore I discovered bed sheets that were being made in lovely patterns and colors. Sew half-a-dozen or more king-size ones together and they would afford privacy from the prying eyes of night wandering deer and racoons. That seemed like a reasonable answer, and it was proffered to Ken when he returned from a business trip to the offices he covered in Malaysia. He was shocked.

"Sheets! Ridiculous! We want something different! How about batik? There's an art director in Kuala Lumpur who designs for a batik factory. Maybe he could do something for us."

My heart sank. I'd seen the local batik and it just wasn't *me*. But, when Ken makes a decision, it's made. Unless I could come up with a better alternative, support it with research, reasoning and conviction, the dye for our curtains was cast. I couldn't and it was. Ismail Mustam, whom I hadn't yet met, was our designer. Ken talked to him, outlined the size of the windows and asked him to draw something.

"What do you want it to be about?" Ismail asked, not unreasonably.

"Oh, fish, turtles, birds, trees, deer, the kind of things that we find there at the lake."

"O. K."

Eventually I got to Kuala Lumpur, met Ismail, a charming man, and saw the design which was bold, striking and beautiful. I picked the colors, warm, varying tones of yellow and brown. We went to the "factory" where the cloth was to be dyed at the invitation of the proprietor, a sultan's grandaughter. It was in a jungle clearing near a small stream. Great swaths of multi-hued cloth were stretched over green foliage. Brown-skinned craftsmen molded tin into intricate patterns.

Women pressed the patterns into wax and then on the cloth, rinsed dyed bolts in the stream, changed drab whites and creams into peacocks of color. It was a slow, painstaking process but we weren't in any hurry. As far as we knew the house wasn't yet under construction! We ordered 50 yards of the 42-inch-wide material, plus the metal patterns. Our curtain material would, indeed be unique. It took, literally, months to make and was slightly damp from its last washing when I packed it in my luggage before flying home. When I got there I found the new balcony railing was a perfect place to drape it to dry. Ken had been right. The curtains, as they are drawn across the window are nothing short of magnificent. Sheets wouldn't have done it.

Circumstances sent me back to the U.S. a full month before Ken's projected return. I headed for home. When I arrived at the lake, after that long time away, the "box for our furniture" that Ken had asked Jerry to construct was a reality. It didn't look at all like just a box, it looked like an integrated and lovely low house in a sort of stairstep arrangement into the side of the hill. From the lake side the window soared and glinted in the sunlight. A stained glass door that was once part of an English pub, shone like a jewel in the west wall. Working with Jerry I made the final decisions about floor coverings. I painted and wallpapered, stained and arranged. The furniture came out of storage and moved in as though it had been made for the place. Everything was more or less finished just one day before Ken arrived at the airport thirty miles away. He had been flying, with no breaks except between-plane waits, for twenty-four hours.

He dozed and I drove, but he was awake as we turned into the drive and slowed between the twin maples.

"It looks wonderful," he said.

I walked him around to the new front door, the stained glass one, and we entered into the big living room. He sat in one of the swinging monkey chairs we had shipped home from Singapore, looked up at the shining brass chandelier, swiveled around to gaze out the huge picture window that framed the lake.

"Wonderful," he repeated.

"Finally," I thought, "we're home for good."

KEN:

That's how Alice remembers it. I hadn't the heart, at that particular moment, to tell her that I had equivocated. Somehow, I wasn't quite ready to let go altogether and had agreed to return to Southeast Asia to work for eight to ten weeks a year for a couple more years. It was a sort of lifeline to the past, to my chosen trade, a chance to slip back into urban ways should the rural life pall. It was checking the bets against possible boredom, leaving a loophole in case of loneliness. Her commitment was total, enthusiastic, heartfelt. Mine was timid and tempered with doubt. We had lived as aliens in strange places and felt homesickness for things and people we knew. Mightn't this very private place that we had created prove to be, for me, another strange land? I really wasn't sure.

7

On Becoming Part of the Community

KEN:

THE GRAVELLED county thoroughfare that passes our entrance is less than a mile in length. Only five families, besides us, claim the same road as part of their addresses. During our part-time living at the lake we got to know some of them well, all of them at least a little bit. During that same period, Ed, our builder, had become a good friend, and, as acquaintances, we had assorted plumbers, electricians, painters, carpenters and merchants in the nearby town. But gone was the large, accustomed urban social apparatus built around lots of neighbors, folks from church, clubs, troops, office colleagues and business acquaintances. For Alice, who grew up far from the maddening crowd, it was a return to normalcy. For me, the challenge was to make new friends, fast. Fate decided to help with the process.

It was undoubtedly just a coincidence, but the addition to our house and our move into it, was completed just as the local Friends of the Library were planning their Fall Home Tour. By further coincidence the lady who was then chief librarian, Eileen Oehler, was simultaneously engaged in a personal search for country property. That quest led her to prowl down our driveway and to stop at our front doorway. Alice, who was weeding, said a civil hello. The librarian reciprocated and then said:

"My, what a lovely house."

Alice promptly invited her to have a look around. The librarian, no shy Marian, got out and stayed more than an hour. She had the full treatment as only Alice, proudly, can give it, plus tea and cookies. A few days later two Home Tour Committee members appeared and Alice did an encore. Before they left, they asked if we would be willing to make our home one of the attractions to be offered when the Fall Home Tour was announced.

It was a good cause, providing funds for book purchases and maintenance. We talked it over between ourselves and with friends and neighbors.

"It means just anyone can walk through your house for the price of a ticket," was one reaction.

"With your collections out where anybody could take anything. Won't you be worried about possible pilfering?" somebody else asked.

We had never thought of things as "collections." There were mementos of excursions at home and abroad. There was an assortment of antique bottles that we'd found in the attic of the 200-year-old stone house on the farm where Alice grew up. A doctor had lived there in the 1870s. The names of various elixirs he had prescribed were etched right into the blue-tinged crystal containers: Magnetic Ointment, Cure for Consumption, Nerve and Bone Liniment, Genuine Essence, and simply Magic Oil were a few of the promises that gleamed in the glass. We thought of them as interesting, not valuable.

"What if it rains?" was another expressed concern.

When we were right down to decision time, we recalled the

pleasure a couple of home tours had given us, how they had inspired some ideas that had become part of our living pattern.

"Besides," Alice said, "It will give us a chance to meet a lot of people." She has a way of getting to the core of things.

As soon as we said yes, we got to know the other people who were opening their own homes for the occasion. Three of the couples were organizers of the town's Great Books Club which we would join within the year.

That led the way to many evenings of lively discussions with very nice, very intelligent people who knew more about the area, its history and folklore, than we could have imagined. Over the years we've mixed discussions of school taxes, downtown development and a new school superintendent with evaluations and analyses of the Book of Revelations, Hemingway's *Farewell to Arms*, Shakespeare's *Timon of Athens* and dozens of other books and plays. There's no cultural lag in our town of 6,900.

One book club member, also a leading industrialist, Stephen Johnson, was concerned about the imminent closing of the only movie house we have. So he bought the place, put it under new management, refurbished the auditorium. He saw that the best and latest films came to town and soon the Cinema was doing better than ever.

Another club member, May Granata, who, until her retirement, taught English in the High School, wrote wonderful, original poems based on the subject books.

Then there's Paul Siegel, who has practiced law in the County for something over thirty years. He tells fascinating stories about the colorful characters who have served on the bench and at the bar.

There's Carolyn Coleman, first lady chairperson of the County Board of Commissioners, and Ken Granata, with a lifetime in police work ranging from the Army's Criminal Investigation Division in Vienna to the local Sheriff's Department. Fascinating people, all, and most of them we might never have known had it not been for the Tour and our participation.

It didn't rain. It was a perfectly gorgeous day and more than two hundred people trooped through our home. Here, verbatim, is the narration delivered by the gracious ladies who conducted visitors through the house:

"The 20 by 30 living room is enhanced by large book shelves and a heatilator fireplace. One wall is covered by paintings of 'places we've been done by people we know' as the Joneses say. A collection of Civil War memorabilia is displayed on rough lumber mantels at the room's north end. Furniture is a combination of antiques collected by the owners and pieces brough back from Singapore and Bangkok. Hanging 'monkey chairs' offer unusual comfort, and an interesting planter's chair once graced the veranda of the Singapore Cricket Club. Displayed on the stair wall is a thirty-star American flag, found in the attic of a Pennsylvania farmhouse.

"Stairs lead to a balcony bedroom and bath. Authentic Victorian furniture is grouped on the balcony. On shelves surrounding it are souvenirs from every corner of the world. A glass sliding door leads from the stair landing into the dining room. Photographs taken by Mr. Jones in Japan, Ireland, Corfu, the Virgin Islands and Thailand decorate one wall adjacent to Mrs. Jones's collection of crystal. Old sleighbells and bells from many parts of the world hang by the fireplace. The furniture is antique."

It all sounded great as the hostesses explained our house to visitors. We shook a lot of hands, saw a lot of people. Nothing from our prized "collections" vanished and everybody seemed to have a wonderful time. When we went to town after the tour we'd get nods and hellos and pleasant comments from folks who might otherwise have been strangers. Little did we know where this first exposure as Public Figures would eventually lead us. Practically immediately Alice was a charter member of the local chapter of the American Association of University Women. She was one of the first ladies in a newly organized hospital guild.

Early on, at the behest of our friend Ed McPharlin, the builder, I got into county politics. Ed got in first. He was irritated by the constant escalation in property taxes, so he started something called the County Taxpayer's League. He ran an ad suggesting that people who felt as he did about taxes come to a meeting. They did. It was, in fact, a real mass meeting, jammed to the doors. Shortly thereafter, Ed ran as a Democrat in a preponderantly Republican area and got elected a county commissioner.

He found it was pretty hard to hold down property taxes under constant pressure from state government so he decided to try some other ways of serving the citizenry. He and I talked some about the fact that few of the then available federal programs had been implemented in our area. I claimed it was because nobody had tried hard enough to take advantage of such programs. He and another commissioner had lunch with me and, between us, we created my first and only, paid, public job, County Grants Coordinator. For a very small salary, an office and telephone, I'd have a chance to put some of Uncle Sam's money where my mouth was.

The first thing learned, the hard way, was that my fellow countians were highly suspicious of U.S. Bureaucrats bearing gifts. They knew, deep down, that long strings were attached to any federal munificence and those strings could strangle independence. As soon as I began consorting with people from HUD (the Department of Housing and Urban Development), I was suspect. When word leaked out that we were trying to set up a housing commission so we could obtain funds for a senior citizen housing complex, suspicions doubled. It was, so some folks said: "an attempt to impose another layer of government on the over-taxed, over directed, and overwrought citizens of Barry County!"

Two prominent ladies were conversing in a local cafe. Overheard, it went like this:

"That new fella, Jones, he's trying to fix things so that Washington can put us right out of our houses and into Projects."

"No!"

"It's true. If you ask me, he's a Communist."

Discouraging words for a new boy trying for community improvement.

Another local housewife decided that our embryo housing commission was illegal. Eventually she took us to court and proved that, on a technicality, she was right. A blow was struck for the democratic process, and our senior citizen housing crumbled beneath it.

Later, by working through a private builder, we were able to resuscitate the project and get the units built. By that time I had been castigated in letters to the editor, yelled at in public hearings and was beginning to understand how local politics and government worked. When apparent strangers glared at me on the streets and nobody sat next to me at the cafe counter I knew I had arrived as a Public Figure.

The difficulties didn't matter that much. These were years when there was generous federal assistance available for local projects. Tax monies could be obtained to help communities solve local problems. Of course there were strings attached, but they were largely to assure accountability. At any rate, after a year of effort, the office of County Grants Coordinator was able to report grants of about $300,000 from HUD, CETA, the state Department of Natural Resources, the state university, the local Community Action Agency and one private foundation.

Some of that money allowed rehabilitation of twenty houses with elderly, low income occupants, homes that were going to ruin simply because there was no money for repairs. They were made decent for the owners and restored to the county's inventory of available housing for future needs.

Other Federal money provided for the development of a beach area in the county park, a place that was enjoyed by some 30,000 visitors each summer.

It opened up a Headstart program for the children of working mothers who couldn't afford private nursery schools, and allowed employment of a county forester whose work would have a considerable effect on the timber resources important to economic development. That forester, Linda Tatum, incidentally, was a Michigan State University graduate in Forestry. It was her first job and the beginning of a distinguished career in her chosen field, so we inadvertently struck a blow for equal employment opportunities.

The job of pulling the funds into the county was fascinating, frustrating and fun. It was a competitive game in which we were pitted against every other county in the nation. The challenge was to prove need, the reward was money. The techniques included proposal writing, on-your-feet presentations, phone calls, lunches, marshaling community support through letter writing, mass meetings, lobbying state and federal legislators and praying.

For tips and guidance I found an instructive book called *Grants—How to Find Out About Them and What to Do Next*. It lists seventeen different and distinct types of grants. It details a computer file of 2,000 institutions that distribute money for hundreds of different purposes. It was a textbook on tapping vast reservoirs of cash.

It was a busy and enlightening fourteen months. According to my original agreement, I then resigned in favor of a young, career-oriented person who would carry on the function permanently. Syd Dulaney took the job and she ran it proudly and successfully until budgets and the political climate eliminated the function.

The deepest kind of philosophic and governmental questions are involved in an examination of the whole grants syndrome. Should small units of government get federal help to better provide for the needs of their communities? Do they, indeed, recognize those needs? Are we really our brothers' keepers or should each person, unless truly handicapped, make his or her own way?

These kind of questions were at the heart of impassioned hearings at which I was sometimes identified with the dark forces of Washington tyranny, creeping socialism, and Marxist philosophy. Often, those who protested most vociferously were, themselves, beneficiaries of veterans' benefits, social security, farm subsidies, unemployment checks or food stamps. Yet they deeply feared big government and possible interference with their individual activities. They wanted life, liberty, the pursuit of happiness and some sort of assistance, too, but without nosiness and interference. Taxes, bureaucrats and politicians of opposite persuasions were identifiable villains, with big business lurking in the background as a fourth force for evil. These are the people who finally speak at the polls and who have, in recent years, supported policies and candidates that are foursquare against "federal handouts." I'm glad I was County Grants Coordinator when the job could be productive.

Then there was the Planning and Zoning Commission on which I served as chairman for two terms. Now that's the way to learn geography. The job required inspection of sites requesting variations from existing ordinances. It took Alice and me down back roads, through swamps, into every township in the county. We met and talked with dozens of citizens who were either for or against what was happening to land in their area.

Some thought commercial development represented progress, others thought it would destroy the rural values and quality of life that they treasured.

The most emotional issue was Mobile Homes. Somehow they became a symbol of the endless struggle between the haves and have-nots, the establishment and the newcomer, the law-and-order folks and the we'll-do-as-we-damn-please people.

As Planning Chairman I was bound to interpret and administer existing ordinances, to uphold them unless and until they were changed by due process. Those ordinances limited the placement of mobile homes to designated parks or for very specific uses. They weren't written to accommodate the people who bought an acre of land and wanted an instant and inexpensive home on it. It turned out that there were quite a lot of such people and their attitude was "it's my land and I can do whatever I want with it." That attitude found a lot of sympathy among citizens who devoutly believe the Jeffersonian statement about the best government being the least government.

In our county that contingent found a Leader, a fiery, stocky, white-haired Libertarian. The fact that he ran a very large mobile home business in an adjoining county may have contributed to his enthusiasm for the cause of the dissidents. They gathered together under a banner that he invented, an organization called OTLAM, an acronym for Outraged Taxpayers and Landowners of Michigan. What a dedicated group they were!

At every meeting of Planning and Zoning, at every public hearing, they were on hand and, at least once, regardless of the agenda, someone would make a speech about the rights of the individual landowner vs the encroachments of governmental authority. When meetings had to be gaveled into some semblance of order you invited headlines in the militant, local paper, heavy black type, too:

JONES CALLED RUDE AND ARROGANT.

Sometimes I felt like George the Third imposing the Stamp Tax for trying to enforce zoning laws, which we were simutaneously trying to rewrite and change in an orderly way. At one point in time, five couples had actually placed their older, second-hand "trailers" on land not zoned for them. They wanted to keep them there, we wanted them moved. Irate neighbors had protested the illegal infringement and requested, nay demanded, enforcement of the ordinance. Eventually we found ourselves in court and our ordinance and actions were upheld against charges of unconstitutionality. A disgruntled OTLAM faded from public view, the ordinances were revised to permit certain types of mobile homes to be placed in approved locations, and life went back to normal for the Planning and Zoning Commission.

Seven years of that, another seven with the Parks and Recreation group, four as chairman of a Committee for Economic Development and nearly two as Grants Coordinator. That's twenty years in local government and we had only really lived in the county for about eight! That's more involvement in public affairs than we had during two dozen years of city dwelling. We've gained a sense of what participatory democracy really means, a feeling that one man and one woman really can make a difference!

For a number of years, once every month Alice would leave the house at 6:00 A.M. and head for Pennock hospital. By 6:30 she would set up shop in the cafeteria there. A table beside her was spread with the most delectable home-baked goodies you can imagine. There were sticky buns and caramel rolls, pies and cookies, tarts and twists and doughnuts. Some she baked herself, others were donations by other guild members. All of it was on sale all morning and all proceeds went to improving the lot of the patients, buying better equipment, enhancing the health care abilities of the community.

Once, and sometimes twice, every week, for ten years, Alice pushed the free library cart through the hospital's halls. It's loaded with everything from Louis L'Amour westerns and Barbara Cartland romances to biographies and how-to books. Current copies of a dozen periodicals are available. She stopped at every door on every floor, except for intensive care units or where there are possibilities of contagion.

"Would you like something to read?" Alice asked.

Answers varied, but more often than not they led to additional conversation. Not just about books, but about illnesses and accidents, children and grandchildren, hopes and dreams and personal histories. My wife is a good listener. Weeks and months later people would nod and smile in a checkout line in the supermarket or at a street corner and we couldn't quite place them. But they certainly seemed to know Alice. She's still The Book Cart Lady, but only once a month now. The hours she used to spend at Pennock Hospital are now spent reading and recording books for the blind and physically handicapped through the Library of Michigan.

There is more than one way to become a public figure. There's more to life, too, than The Job, that all encompassing entity that once absorbed so much energy. There is Community, visible and active all around us. Time sharing, here, involves unhurried conversation on a street corner in town, or over a fence line nearer home. Friends come fishing or drop off a dozen precious morel mushrooms found in a nearby woods. Even disagreements, and there have been some of those, are more personal and involving than they ever used to be.

We're more concerned with persons than we used to be, and less surrounded by people.

A big event in Hastings is the annual Summerfest, held in

August, and the Parade that's part of it. For four years now, we've rolled out Groucho, our restored 1954 DeSoto, shined it up, and taken our place in line. The past summer, the lovely, vivacious Nahlik twins, Susie and Sandy, from Missouri, were visiting on Parade Day. We were Number Three in line, right behind the Grand Marshal. As we rode along the twins heard people shout:

"It's the Joneses. Hi, Alice, Hi, Ken. Who are the pretty girls?"

The twins could tell we were, indeed, surrounded by persons.

8

On Neighbors

KEN:

THE SAME WORD can mean different things, depending on where you grew up. Take "neighbors." To me, as a kid, they were the people who lived on either side of us, with a six-foot gangway between houses. My mother and Mrs. Hoffman always nodded hello and were pleasant to each other when they happened to emerge from their respective front doors simultaneously. The fact that our lives related to theirs was sheer coincidence and leave it at that. If, perchance, a few neighbors eventually became friends, that was an unexpected bonus.

Oddly, the closer the neighbors, the more they kept their distance. For example, in a downtown apartment where Alice and I once lived along with hundreds of other tenants, I sometimes felt like a ghost. In the elevator people seemed to look through you rather than at you. Eye contact was rare and brief. One never spoke to strangers in the carpeted hallways, or if one did, any response was likely to be monosyllabic at best.

Once there was an exception, but that involved our dog,

Robin, more than it did me. The prized poodle and I were returning from a walk around the neighborhood one brisk winter's eve. As we strolled down the corridor a large, rather elegant, lady came towards us. Our paths had crossed before but never with any acknowledgement. This was different. Her face lit up, aglow with friendliness. As she came abreast of us she stooped and said:

"Ooooh, there's a new doggy on the floor."

Robin wagged, and had her ears scratched in return

"Hims a pretty thing. Would hims like to meet my little man?"

For all the attention I was getting I could have been a post at the end of the leash that connected me with the pup. I made a bid to be noticed

"Madam," I said, "I'm with her."

"Oh, you're a female are you," the lady still addressed Robin directly. "Well I certainly hope you've been fixed."

And off she went, still without a word to me.

I suppose when hundreds of people are cheek to jowl and the walls are thin, and the pressures great, there's something to be said for self-imposed isolation. It seems like a sorry substitute for the neighborliness, the involvement, the human feelings that go with life on the backroads.

That's the life that Alice had lived. For one thing most of her childhood neighbors were aunts, uncles, cousins and grand-parents. For another, there was always time to talk and visit. Neighbors, indeed, were the people you knew best and cared about most. That's something that I have had to learn.

One teacher was our neighbor, Charlie. He and his wife, Celia, enriched our lives immeasurably during our first years at the farm. Charlie was a raconteur without peer and I found out that listening to him was never a waste of time. He used marvelous phrases like "a blacksnaky kind of day" to describe a hot August afternoon. When he said it you could see the serpent lazily sunning itself on a rock at the water's edge. His powers of recall were phenomenal. When he recounted the tale of a long-ago tornado that he and some companions had watched from a sheltering barn it made you shiver. The sky blackened, the wind's moan became a roar and you cowered in a corner as part of the roof went. Things happened all over again when Charlie told about them.

There was the hard winter when he saddled up his horse and started across a frozen lake to run some trap lines. As he neared the shoreline the ice buckled and cracked and he and his mount were pitched into the frigid water. It was shallow enough for them to flounder out but the wind was blowing, the temperature nearing zero, and it was a long way to home.

"I was so tired from threshing around in that water," the story went, "that I just flopped down on the horse's neck, held on, and let him get us home. When we got there, they had to chop me off."

Trapping played a big part in the young farm boy's start. Married, and with a family started, he did anything and everything to eke out a living. That included running trap lines for his older brother. For his work he got four dollars a day, a heavy coat and rubber boots. Pelts were going for a dollar and a quarter and some days he would bring in a hundred rats.

"We'd stack 'em in a corner five and six feet high," he recalled, "and it would take until two in the morning to skin 'em."

After he figured the sizable proceeds, Charlie decided to rent his own trapping grounds. He paid a taciturn neighbor twenty dollars for rights to a pond that hadn't been available to anyone else for ten years. In his first season that, and some nearby streams, yielded 738 pelts. The First World War then in progress sent the price of furs skyrocketing and muskrat furs were up to four and five dollars.

"My father always told me that trappers were a no-count breed," the old man chuckled. "They lived in tumbledown cabins with a donkey in the dooryard and hounds all around, he said. So when I bought my first eighty acres and a little house off him I had the laugh. Fifteen hundred dollars of the payment came right off the trapline."

Hard cash was scarce and the quest for it took Charlie to the woods to fell the giant oaks and maples, the hickories and walnuts that timber buyers wanted. He acquired a threshing machine and did custom work for farmers near and far. His working days were sixteen hours and more, and once he was into the dairy business, there weren't any holidays.

His first eighty acres became a hundred and sixty, then two hundred and eventually nearly five hundred acres of farmland, timber, swamp and lake. He walked and knew every inch of it and for every turn there was a tale to tell. We listened to them in the warm kitchen that Ceil kept, redolent always with cooking and baking smells, stopping place for a steady stream of friends and relatives who always found the time to visit, listen and talk.

Sometimes Charlie would open with a statement like:

"I'll bet I'm the only feller you ever knew that was run over by a stagecoach."

Incontrovertibly, he was.

That would lead to a description of the long-vanished Pritchardville crossroads store where a stage stopped, and a baby who crawled into the muddy road just as the conveyance rolled by.

"If it hadn't been soft I might have been hurt, but I just sunk into the mud. My mother had a time cleaning me up."

Charlie and I fished the lake together. One winter I ran his trap line with him. Disregarding his warning I took a shortcut and went over my boot tops into a hidden spring. He laughed so hard he had to sit on a stump to get his breath.

He told me how to sow clover in the winter on the snow. Half-doubting, I tried it. The spring melt carried the seed deep into the earth and when summer came the white and purple blossoms testified to the old man's wisdom. He walked the woods with me and showed me bee trees and dens and forest giants that were hollow inside. He told me the tricks of timber buyers and the personality traits of cows. He educated me in many ways. It was a sad day when he and I had a falling out over cows and pasture rights and a vague agreement for his use of my land.

Celia and Alice tried to patch it up but we were both stubborn and things were never the same. Celia and Charlie are gone now and we miss them both. They were good neighbors. Sometimes, when walking a fence line or tilling the garden, I look up and almost see the old man's spare, long-striding form coming over a distant hill. He'll stop, when he gets to me, and tell me another story.

Just across the road and west of our mailbox there's an old farmhouse that's been restored to beauty and usefulness. Charlie's daughter, Donna, and her husband, George Cullers, live there. Donna's life has been a saga of adversity overcome and happiness found. She had a troubled first marriage which ended and left her with three children to raise, one of whom was severely handicapped. She went to work on a production line, earned her and her children's way until a daughter was married and a son off to war in Vietnam. She sought the best medical care and advice in a vain quest to save her other child, but it wasn't possible. Through it all she maintained a bounce and ebullience that were amazing. Just when it looked like her next problem might be loneliness, along came George. A country boy from West Virginia he loved the same things she did. They hunted together, fished, went to bluegrass music festivals. They laughed a lot, fought some. Both had been through tough previous marriages and they were a little loath to try again. Finally they did and now their house is a constant beehive of activities as his children and hers, and their grandchildren come and go. There are cattle in the fields and chickens in the chicken house and Donna's kitchen is as warm and as peopled as was her mother Celia's.

Another blessing, during our first years at the Lake, was Mel Beach, from just down the road. Whatever broke, he could fix. Whatever needed building, he could build. When we were away he kept an eye on things. If grass needed cutting, it got cut.

The hourly rates we paid him could never cover the value of his help and concern.

Our nearest neighbors, the Granatas, we've mentioned earlier. They had actually preceded us as purchasers of part of what had once been the Van Vranken farm. Their home had been the original farmhouse. The eleven acres around it, as well as our land, was all part of a homestead that dated back to the Blackhawk War. What they found, originally, was a decrepit, neglected building and a yard full of debris. Although the words "sweat equity" hadn't been thought of at the time, that's what May and Ken invested in the rehabilitation of what is now a truly lovely building. The things they had already learned about plumbers, electricians, carpenters they gladly shared with us. Our first rowboat on the lake was an old, metal-bottomed monster that had been stored in their barn. The second craft in our growing fleet was a ponderous float boat that had served as a work vessel at a nearby marina. Ken Granata located it. As a member of the county Sheriff's department he got around a lot. He, too, had stories to tell. Some were about Vienna where he had been a member of the army's Criminal Investigation Division during the four-power occupation right after World War II. Others dated back to his youth in the Bronx, to days aboard the luxury liners of Cunard where he served as a steward to movie stars and tycoons.

Like most good law enforcement people he had little to say about the things that happened day-to-day. Once, though, I caught a glimpse. It was winter and the roads were ice-slicked and it was his day off. He was visiting me when the phone rang. Hearing his ring on our party-line telephone, Ken answered. It was the sheriff's office calling. All other available officers were on assignments and a call had come in from a county resident. The road below his house had been flooded and frozen over. Now there was a car, half submerged, sitting in the middle of the drowned area, fifty yards beyond a sign that said ROAD UNDER WATER. Would Officer Granata go and investigate? He would. Because it would be quicker I offered to drive him to the scene in my front-wheel-drive car, built to negotiate the kind of slick roads that were waiting for us. It took us about twenty minutes to get there. The ice was thick enough to walk on, but too thin to handle the weight of the car that had broken through. Ken preceded me, peered through the frosted windows. He turned, his face grim.

"Go to the nearest house and call headquarters," he told me. "There are people in here."

I stayed around until other officers arrived and removed the frozen bodies of a man, a woman and a child. They were like marble, white and still. I had a better idea, then, of what it must take to be a policeman.

May, Ken's wife, had devoted her life to teaching literature, poetry, theatre. She taught English in the local high school and brought innovations as well as erudition to the job. She organized theatre parties to nearby cities, obtained movies of Shakespeare's plays, opened the eyes and minds of students as few educators ever do.

Those are the people whose lives and property lines have been and are closest to ours. Other families live along our rough and graveled road and we've watched their children grow, seen them at our annual Christmas Open House, joined them on deer drives.

There have been rough spots, disagreements, misunderstandings, of course. In the country, somehow, they seem to cut deeper, last longer and hurt more. Once you've been through a reasonless, or contrived rural vendetta you see the Martins and the Coys as a true tragedy, not a hillbilly farce. When you come out the other side of a foolish feud, you've grown up a little, too."

Amazingly, trouble and all, you know that should any need arise these neighbors would be on hand to help in any way they could and maybe that's what civilization is really all about. Maybe that feeling is more important than the conveniences, comforts, entertainments, prestige and effortlessness; the superficiality and guardedness of the cities.

An absentee owner is proprietor of the land just south of us. For a long time he was a stranger. Along his fence line are neat, wooden signs that say NO TRESPASSING − WILDLIFE REFUGE. Hundreds of acres in the county are thus protected and according to the plat book they all belong to Doc B. During deer season, a jeep patrols the perimeters to discourage poachers. The owner himself has never been a visible presence; about the only reference to him is late in hunting season when discouraged nimrods can be heard to mutter:

"The deer are all holed up on the Doc's land."

So, when a friend asked me to help with a fund drive for a nearby Nature Center and it turned out that the drive chairman was Doctor Lewis Batts, I accepted. Here was a chance to meet the man behind the name in the plat book. It turned out that Doctor Batts is one of the nation's outstanding conservationists, founder and director of the nearby Kalamazoo Nature Center, advocate of energy conservation, former professor, writer and visionary. I worked with him for a number of months, Alice and I joined the Nature Center and it has enriched our lives, given us a greater appreciation for things all around us.

Once, among the myriad activities announced by the center, a bird walk to be conducted by the Doc was listed. It would be in a remote area and a number of ornithological experts would be along to help identify species through sight and sound. It sounded good so we signed up for it.

Departure time was to be at 6:00 A.M. from the Nature Center, an hour's drive from our house, which meant that reveille that morning would sound at 4:30 A.M. That didn't faze me a bit, especially after I found out that business would require my presence in New York that day.

"But don't let that stop you," I urged Alice, "Take a friend."

So she lined up a lovely young friend, Agnes Karas, who has a passion for birds, picked her up at 5:00 A.M., and they were in plenty of time for the van that was to haul eleven enthusiasts to the announced "remote area."

The Doc welcomed Alice. He smiled, quizzically.

"You won't need to go in the van," he said. "We'll be walking just the other side of your property line."

It was about 7:30 A.M., three hours after the wake-up time, when Alice parked her car about a quarter of a mile from home and followed the naturalist through the splendid woods just across our back line fence. They saw and heard more than forty different species. I suspect that about half of them had taken nourishment at the bird feeders on our back porch.

Once, by arrangement, I met the doc at the line fence that separates our properties. That turned out to be the start of something exciting. He had come over at my request to look at some trees along the line that I wanted to remove in order to improve the fence. He agreed that they could be spared and then, at my invitation, he hopped over the wire and we took a walk towards the lake. He was interested in every bush, plant, weed, rock, every roll in the terrain, every pothole or hillock. When we were almost to the water he stopped and looked off to the east.

"I'd like to have a closer look at that," he pointed.

That was a large and unusual tree which delighted us every May. It would break out with a cloud of white blossoms when most other trees were barely in bud.

From our dining room it looked like an earthbound cloud.

Close up, you could see that there were dozens of large shoots extending upward from the sizable trunk. It looked like a banyan tree in reverse.

Doc B. walked over to take a closer look. He circled it, he backed off and eyed its height.

"It could be a state champion," he surmised.

Until then I had never realized that trees were competitive.

"Mind if I tell the Kalamazoo Garden Club about it?" he asked.

A few weeks later, two pleasant ladies and their interested husbands came over with tape measures. They were participants in the Big Tree Hunt, an ongoing event with Garden Club support throughout the country.

They got pretty excited about our tree. Next thing you know, an extraordinary educator from the Cranbrook Institute in Bloomfield Hills, Michigan, showed up with an instrument for measuring height. He wasn't a demonstrative type, but he seemed impressed. So were we when a letter from Dr. Paul Thompson arrived a few weeks later:

Dear Mr. Jones:

Your shadbush tree is a state champion—almost a national champion. It scores a total of 158 points whereas the national champ has 165. It has a good chance in the future of becoming national champion. The girth is 78 inches, Ht. 62 ft and spread 70 ft. I am enclosing a Big Tree sign for the tree. In mounting it, leave the nails protruding about one-half inch to allow for tree growth.

With best regards

Paul Thompson.

The sign has been duly installed. The tree, known variously as a shadbush, juneberry or serviceberry, seems oblivious of its fame.

For two years it was listed as national champion on the Register of Big Trees maintained by *American Forests Magazine.* We proudly found it among "Giant Trees of the U.S." in the *1985 World Almanac* listed as "Serviceberry, Downy—Height 63 ft.—1984—Barry County, Mich." Now it's an inch or two more around, a foot higher and spreads four feet farther than it did when this all started. It rates 161 points. I don't know what happened to to the former king, the tree that rated 165 points. I guess it became, literally, a fallen champion. Though we certainly did nothing to deserve it, we couldn't help but feel proud as we gazed across the lake at our truly distinguished fellow resident.

But fame is fleeting. In 1987 we received a rather terse communication from the American Forestry Association.

"Please be advised that the champion (161 points) has been 'dethroned.' A 181-point tree located in Virginia has surpassed this champ in measurement, and is now the new champion."

Long live the King.

When spring comes our tree looks as regal as ever to us.

Up the road and around the corner lives Forest Halleck, a solitary man. His home is the old house where he has lived, boy and man, almost all of his life. He was away during World War II, returned, looked after his parents until their deaths, then settled down to something like a hermit's existence. He cuts cordwood and sells it off the acreage that once was farmland and is now mostly woods. He's been a good friend to us, coming by three or four times a year to visit. We stop by his place with pies, cakes, cookies after Alice has done some baking. He has brought us beautiful huckleberries from the swamp, puffball mushrooms as big as basketballs, a crockery butterchurn that his mother used.

He has concord grapes and makes wonderful wine from a recipe of his own. It has a hint of honey in its bouquet. A big bear of a man nearly always dressed in denim overalls and jackets, Forest peers at the world through thick glasses and isn't too pleased with much that he sees. His favorite books are Louis L'Amour westerns, where lines are clear cut and the heroes are quite distinct from the villains. He prefers the simple life and his is as basic as it can be. Do not think, however, that he is uncivilized. His civility and delicacy are remarkable. Once, during our early years here, Alice wanted to plant some ginseng. As country people know, its root is a powerful curative, a possible aphrodisiac, a substance almost mystical in its properties.

She had obtained, from a catalog, some for planting. I believed neither in the efficacy of this ancient nostrum, nor in the advisability of sticking some in our ground. However, one weekend, reluctantly, I accompanied her, shovel in hand, to a distant hillside, where she thought the stuff might prosper. Keeping up a constant grumble about other, more important things that I should be doing, I set about digging holes wherein she could place the potent plants. Just as I was muttering about how my time at the typewriter was worth a lot more than these minutes at manual labor, Alice blew her stack. For a person her size she has powerful pipes.

"WHY DON'T YOU STOP TRYING TO LAY A GUILT TRIP ON ME?" she yelled. Before I could reply she continued, fortissimo: "THIS WAS SUPPOSED TO BE FUN!"

I stuttered something, but not much.

"IF YOU DON'T WANT TO HELP AND ENJOY IT, JUST GO ON HOME."

I was taken aback. She added a little and I believe I may have apologized, because her voice returned to normal. Little did we know that in his woods, nearby, friend Forest was stacking logs.

Weeks later while talking to Alice and he casually said:

"My, but you do have a carrying voice."

That's all. He certainly hadn't been eavesdropping, but if you holler loud enough, your neighbors can't help hearing. Since then, we've kept our outdoor disagreements below the echo point.

Sometimes I wish that a time machine could transport me to the early 1900s to see this land as it once was. From what old-timers like Forest and Charlie have said far more of it was culti-vated back when horses pulled the plows. Those were the days when "family farm" meant exactly that; when a big garden, a milk cow, a few pigs and a flock of chickens provided much of what was needed; when it was usual for three generations to live under a single roof.

Today those roofs sag from age, much of the pasture and garden land has gone back to brush, and only a few aging people like Forest and the Burpee boys linger to recall the good yesteryears.

Ken and Bill Burpee are well past fifty and they live in a vast, ramshackle farm house not far away. As it shelters them, so it sheltered their parents and grandparents. Kenneth is a regular visitor on bee business, another result of Alice's proclivity for reading ads in the local paper. This one was headed: BEEHIVES FOR SALE.

"Let's get them," she said.

"Why do you want them?" I asked, not unreasonably.

"Daddy kept bees," she answered. "When I was little I used to put a drop of sugar water on my finger and the bees would come and drink it."

"That's the nuttiest thing I ever heard of," was my reply.

"Wouldn't it be nice to have our own honey?" Alice asked."

So we acquired two decrepit wooden boxes of extremely active honeymakers.

The old hives were termite infested and repair work was urgently needed. Alice told Forest and Forest, who had been a beekeeper, knew Kenneth Burpee and sent us to see him and, thus, he became our bee man. Personally, I would just as soon buy my sweet stuff all jarred and ready, and only help with the bees when dragooned into it by my fearless wife.

Mostly, the busy little creatures are the wards of Alice and Kenneth. When they get ready to extract their annual tribute from the hives Alice suits up in helmet, net, gauntlets, coveralls tied down at ankle and wrist. Kenneth puts a paper bag over his head, drapes a face net from it and, barehanded, with no other protection, goes to work. Alice handles the smoker that stuns the bees, Kenneth removes supers, brushes off bees and proceeds, methodically, to do what has to be done. I watch from a distance. Over the years the hives have produced their own dramas. Once, a queen died, leaving her subjects confused and purposeless. Within days the aggressive, motivated bees from the other colony started attacking the listless workers in the deprived hive and stealing honey from it. Until Kenneth came over we didn't know what was wrong. Post haste we sent for another queen, inserted her into the colony, and restored it to vigorous activity.

Once, after a day away, I came home in the late afternoon. Alice was standing a few feet from the beehives, arm outstretched. In her hand was a tiny jar lid, filled with sugar water. Bees were drinking from it.

Another spring, after an exceptionally long, cold winter, one hive didn't come alive as the weather warmed in late April. When Kenneth came over, on call, we opened it and found catastrophe inside. Every bit of honey was gone, eaten by desperate bees facing starvation. There simply hadn't been enough, and extinction was the result.

In her remorseless way, Nature taught us one lesson. The

second lesson came from Kenneth. Now, if circumstances demand it, we know how to use granulated sugar at the hive entrance to provide subsistence.

They have all been our teachers, neighbors with skills we can never fully master.

Laurel, the pump man, Cliff, the carpenter, Loyal, the mechanic, Jim, the repairman, Bill, the painter, Bert, the electrician, Doug, the plumber, Jack, the landscaper, Russ, the builder, Paul, always on call; the list is long and vital to our well-being. Willard and Dixie, Joyce, Warren, all, and so many more have answered our various calls for advice and assistance.

Without them our lives would be far more difficult. They are the friendly faculty in the complex college of practical knowledge that we continue to attend. While they never grade us, we hope they've noticed some improvement in our self-sufficiency, some growth in our willingness to accept things as they are, and to abide by that best of rural rules, the Golden one.

9

Tools of
the Trade

KEN:

WHEN WE were first married and bought a log house in the foothills of the Ozarks, my farmer father-in-law gave me a present. It was a shiny, green tool box filled with the basics. T-square, hammer, screwdrivers, both regular and Phillips, pliers, brace and bit, enough to get me going as a homeowner. Now I was equipped for the big job of installing some storm windows, each one different, for a highly individual set of windows. The only way to secure the storms was with slip bolts that would slide into holes drilled in the logs. As anybody knows you drill holes with a brace and bit and, thanks to Alice's dad, I had that. So, whistling, I went to work. The logs, although pine, seemed extremely *hard*. I turned and turned and scarcely made a dent. I sweated. I swore. Neither seemed to forward my progress. Alice, hearing me mutter came to watch. After a moment, softly, she said:

"Try turning it from left to right instead of from right to left."
Then she did right and left.

In two hours the whole job was done. She tried not to look smug, and I tried not to look sheepish; but it wasn't easy for either of us.

How an inept tool user and mechanical moron like me could decide on the bucolic life defies imagination. With all the help and assistance one can muster, a place in the country is still, largely, a do-it-yourself domain. To accomplish what must be accomplished you need skills, patience, physical strength and mechanical ingenuity. Outside of a reasonable amount of muscle, I was sorely lacking. Of course I did have Alice, looking over my shoulder, offering needed, but usually resented, counsel. Just because her dad knew how to do practically everything!

My determination to prove myself must have sent chills of horror cavorting down her vertebrae. There was the time I decided to, single-handedly, meet the requirements of The Land Plan. One unequivocal directive stated: "26 acres will be kept open by mowing."

The area in question was covered with brush, small trees, big weeds and tough native grasses. You could hire someone with the necessary equipment to do the job at something like $35 an hour. It would take at least ten hours. Probably have to be done twice a year. Besides that there were other areas that needed work. Solution: Buy a Tractor.

Never mind the fact that you've never even done standard maintenance on the cars you've owned, that you didn't understand the engines on your son's model airplanes. Buy a brush-hog, too, a huge, nasty, five-foot blade that can cut through a two-inch tree if needs be.

Buy a tractor and a brush-hog and do-it-yourself.

At the local implement dealer's we settled on a Japanese-made Satoh, a 4-cylinder tractor, just big enough to operate the hog. I got twenty minutes of instruction and an operating manual, apparently written in Japan. It included some quaint phrasing:

"After the engine has been started, keep off your hand from the starter switch."

Try this one:

"Towing operation should be always made so that setting of an implement be on lower position from the center line of the rear wheel axle." Huh?

After the whole rig was delivered, instruction book in hand, I began to practice in a fairly flat field east of the house. Sitting high on the tractor seat, with the power takeoff engaged and the brush-hog blade whirring its way through weeds and brush, I gained a definite sense of power.

I was kept from overconfidence by fairly regular stories in the rural papers with headlines like:

FARMER DRAGGED TO DEATH BY RUNAWAY TRACTOR

or

NEIGHBORS SAVE MAN PINNED UNDER OVERTURNED TRACTOR

To this day I am a little queasy on steep hillsides, and I try never to overextend the capabilities of the tough little Satoh. Together we've cleared a lot of brush. Now Alice can watch me work with equanimity. I didn't know that for the first month of brush hogging she listened with dread to the whining, growling, crashing sounds of me at work. She listened, without comment, as I read from the detailed, if stilted, service manual. There were lessons in lubrication, maintenance and operation.

It was, you might say, the first in a long line of textbooks. On a shelf near Alice's kitchen cabinet desk there's a file that has grown more rapidly than anything we've planted, fertilized and cultivated. This overstuffed folder contains warranties, guarantees, instructional manuals, diagrams, sketches of circuitry, operating directions, cautionary notes, accessory availabilities, testimonials, and varied bits of advertising puffery. Most of these documents relate to one or the other of the nearly forty engines now on the premises.

There are electrically powered appliances that do an incredible number of jobs. Not just expected things like freezing food, whipping cream, sucking up dust, keeping time and pumping water to house and barn. One durable electric motor operates from the first freezeover of the lake to the time when the ice sings and cracks and thaws for the final time. It activates the Zoeller bubbler that creates the equivalent of a flowing spring in our dock area all winter long.

This creates an open water area ten feet in diameter as a warm current from the bottom circulates and prevents ice from forming at the top. Regardless of pitiless day-after-day cold there's never a shore-to-shore shield shutting all oxygen out of the lake. So fish that might otherwise suffocate, live. Now a companion piece, called a Pondmaster, helps with the oxygenation job. It's only source of power is the wind which turns aluminum blades and a shaft that revolves a subsurface propeller. This also rotates warmth upward preventing ice from forming. Two very necessary and serviceable devices that accomplish a useful purpose without much maintenance and are virtually trouble free.

That "virtually" is a hedge. Once we had eighty-mile an hour winds that stripped the shaft right out of the Pondmaster and dropped the propeller right to the muddy bottom. We needed another winter's ice to provide a footing for repair work. The Bubbler, too, managed to get twisted and turned until the heavy pump separated from its float and sank a foot deep into muck.

Roll up your sleeve and reach six feet down in icy water. Hoist fifteen pounds of cold metal up and out. Put it back together with screwdriver and pliers while you whistle "I'm Just a Country Boy" between chattering teeth.

Outside of a few painful moments like those, the electrical stuff has been, in computer-age language, "user-friendly."

But not so my internal combustion engine collection. From the tiny 21cc hummer on the John Deere Trimmer-Hedger, to the huge, eight cylinder hemi on our restored '54 DeSoto, they are a frustrating family of quarrelsome kids. If only I could hear them all at once, humming, purring, buzzing, burbling, rumbling, each with its own sweet song, it would beat Beethoven done by the London Symphony.

Alas, such a symphony will never sound. When the ailing 17 horsepower garden tractor is cured by a replaced sparkplug, the usually hale Jeep truck starts to cough. It's a minor complaint, a perforated muffler, but it must be treated promptly. Drive around town with that consumptive racket and you're inviting the sheriff's department to pull you over and issue a warning.

Treatment of mechanical maladies is difficult for the amateur and diagnosis is even worse. Why has that which roared into action yesterday and did its appointed tasks with nary a murmur, why has it fallen silent today? An infinitesimal fleck of rust in the gas line, an almost indiscernible break in a wire? It could be those. Or it could be a piece of inadvertent, but monumental, stupidity. Like the time the contents of the kerosene can were poured into the tractor's gasoline tank. Or the car door was left ajar so the dome light burned all night. Or the valve on the outboard was not quite closed and a tankful of fuel dribbled into the lake.

Another way to court catastrophe is by hurrying. One has a definite tendency to do that when the wind-chill is around minus twenty and the snow is drifting the three-hundred yards of driveway shut. It's hard to be deliberate in searching for an oil plug that, somehow, fell from the engine block and hid in the white stuff. So, you take a chance and head for the barn, plugless. Once inside, and warm, a solution can be found. Halfway home the hole stopped gouting engine blood. Another twenty feet and an ominous clatter preceded disaster. The pistons froze faster than a car door keyhole with ice in it. Profanity is pointless, tears would only congeal on the cheeks. Get the Jeep and a tow chain, haul the cripple into harbor and smile when you pay the $141.58 it takes to repair the damage. In the spring, after the thaw, you find the elusive plug right where it dropped out.

Adage for amateur mechanics: *carry patience in your tool box*.

Take time to find what's lost, to fit things properly, to read the manual, to think everything through completely. Completely, I repeat.

Almost doesn't cut it. There was the time the propeller on the floatboat was almost fixed. A shear pin had broken and the boat had to be manuevered into shallow water where it was possible to wade and work. Propeller removed, shear pin replaced.

Whoops! A small cotter pin behind the propeller slipped and fell into the drink. No matter, when the motor ran, the propeller, in effect, just screwed itself on tighter. We could run the boat back to the dock and find a replacement pin. All aboard, start the engine, and away we go back out into the lake. Whoops, again! In reverse the propeller unscrews itself. After fifteen minutes of surface diving I realized that a new propeller ($17) would be required. Alice was sympathetic, but amused.

"Reminds me of the brace and bit," she said.

Let me say that she has always remembered her contribution to the installation of our first storm windows, and it is not an untold tale.

If she were to write another adage for amateurs it would probably be: *don't try to fool the rules.*

Like one time we were taking the Jeep truck up to the big woods to bring back a load of firewood. She asked:

"Sure you got enough air in the tires?"

I gave it the quick visual check and, despite a noticeable soft spot in the left rear doughnut, assured her that all was well. Later, while I was loading, she went to gather watercress from the springs. When the truck was full to capacity and then some I eased it back along the trail. She was walking back towards me and waved. It wasn't a casual wave, it was frantic and she was shouting and pointing. The rear vision mirror showed why.

Smoke was drifting behind me and the bumps now apparent weren't in the terrain. The left rear tire was flat. At my suggestion Alice walked home. Supervision wasn't necessary.

Have you ever jacked up a half-ton truck carrying a three-quarter ton load? Wrestled with a spare tire that's slung underneath the cargo area and held there by a rusty bolt?

No wonder there's so much character written in the faces of old mechanics and farmers.

When the truck had been emptied and its load stacked, I checked the spare and the other wheels with a tire gauge. Pressure was about 24 pounds all around. The directions say, when loaded, carry 30 pounds. Later the local garage man gave me the good news. The flat tire was repairable, no holes in it.

Just overloaded and underinflated, he said. That's all.

Don't try to fool the rules.

Now I have an air compressor to keep the thirty-one tires upon which I depend properly inflated for their respective loads.

The green toolbox is rusty and dented and is still in service although most of the original tools have been mislaid, broken, loaned out or worn out. But what an army of additions has joined the replacements. Skilsaws, chainsaws, and long-handled hook saws for trimming trees; power drills and power sprayers; socket wrench sets, jumper cables, battery checkers and battery chargers; wire cutters, fence stretchers, crow bars, axes, wedges, mauls, an endless array of specialized tools for specialized jobs. There are shelves of magic fluids, too, starter fluids, brake fluids, transmission fluids, windshield washing fluids, a lake of stuff.

To house all this and the seven vehicles, sailboat and sundries, we added a fifty by twenty foot garage to the original mobile home, roofed and sided the whole thing and have a combined guest house and garage that was never part of any plan. That complex and its contents gives us a sense of self-sufficiency that one would never find in an apartment. We feel a sense of kinship with those engineers, mechanics, maintenance people who are so adept at altering environments, at making hostile places into hospitable homelands.

It's nice for a person who has customarily dealt in abstracts to deal with the concrete. It's restful and reassuring to leave the typewriter or word processor to repair the overactive pump that needs adjusting. When, due to your tinkering, the pressure drops from an unacceptable ninety pounds to the prescribed forty you feel a certainty that no carefully wrought sentence or paragraph can ever give you. There's a feeling that whatever comes along, you can handle it.

Sure enough, it does come along. Like the time it was. . . .

The first of January.

Start with a couple of coincidences. After ten years without one, we bought a portable generator. Not because of some im-

minent need, really, but because we could pick up a demonstra-
tor at a savings of three hundred dollars. It sat in the garage,
squat, efficient-looking. Once every two weeks I would pull the
rope starter and it would cough into roaring life.

Then there was the matter of New Year's Eve. More often
than not it meant a forty-mile trip to the city, drinking, dining,
dancing, revelry until midnight. Then another hour of well-wish-
ing and the long, long journey home. This year, however, our
neighbors, Donna and George, invited us to a small get-together
and we accepted.

Business had taken me away from home that December 31st
and in the late afternoon, as I was returning, the ice started to
form. Defrosters kept the windshield clear and there was enough
traffic to keep roads from glazing. The radio carried weather reports that included traveler's advisories, but nothing dire was
predicted. Nevertheless a second trip that day was cancelled and
I snuggled up by my warm word processor as Mother Nature
wound up for some real hardball.

Sibilant, scudding sleet whispered warnings on the windows,
but the real threat was silent. On trees, wires, along roof edges,
on driveways and road surfaces, crystal hard ice was building.
When it was party time, it was all the Jeep could do to scramble
up the hill to the county road. We turned it around and parked it
in the driveway, headed back toward the house. We covered the
windshield with cardboard to keep it clear and, on foot, slid
across the road and down another little hill to Donna's house.

"Happy New Year, neighbors," she greeted us as we doffed
snowmobile suits and boots.

"Happy New Year," called Dwight and Mary Newton, Jack
and Diane Phillips. These hearty celebrants had made their way
the ten miles from town to join the party. Drinking was deliberate, conversation easy and low key, about country things: other
famous storms, deer drives, old-timers, fur trapping. There were
other good stories, well-told, about canoe trips to Canada, rois-
tering in Hong Kong, gambling in Las Vegas. Farmers and rural
folk are great travelers when work permits. Just before midnight

Donna served spicy nachos. Then, on TV, we watched the Times Square crowd greet another round of the seasons as we exchanged kisses and handshakes. With the coming year properly saluted attention turned to what was happening.

"Better run your bathtub full of water," someone suggested.

"Time to hit the road," said another.

By 12:30 the Jeep was garaged and we were drawing water. At 1:10 A.M. the lights went out. Flashlights were at hand, as were emergency candles. We stoked up the wood stove and crawled into bed. Under the blankets and big, down comforter it was fine. Outside, the wind rattled the crusty tree limbs like the bones of a quaking skeleton. In the distance huge branches crashed to the ground, felled by ten million capricious raindrops turned to crystal.

It was still a pitch dark world when we awoke. By candlelight we searched out our coal oil lamp and its orange glow soon suffused the kitchen. A tea kettle sang on the wood stove and, after cold cereal and hot coffee, we were ready to step out into the frozen morning. As we moved through the house we kept flicking switches out of habit and grinning ruefully when nothing happened. The little transistor radio had informed us that 300,000 people were in the same boat, without power. Many had no heat, dependent as they were on electrical ignition and blower systems. Emergency shelters were being opened in the churches and legion halls of nearby towns.

It was easy to see why. The power line into our house drooped under the weight of a solid half-inch of ice encasing the wire. The big Russian olive tree near the house was split and fallen, riven by its own weighted branches. Every so often, somewhere, another tree would fall, making instant thunder followed by the tinkle of shattered ice hitting the sheeted ground. First light showed cedars bent and crouched like giant, immobile bears. There was an awful beauty about it that almost excused the cruelty of the morning. One could only imagine deer and rabbits foraging against the diamond hard surface. Every weed, every bush, seed pod, blade of grass was encased in crystal.

We got busy at the bird feeders and, immediatly, chickadees were plunging into the hanging mason jar that held sunflower seed. Juncos, johnny bulls, goldfinch and chipping sparrows darted to the big, converted street light dome that was the central spot for mixed seeds. A bully of a bluejay attacked an ear of corn. Downy woodpeckers drilled at a frozen peanut butter mixture, or hung upside down from an old onion bag, pecking at the suet it contained. Our flying friends would survive as long as the stations were manned.

Now to take care of ourselves. The portable generator, so fortuitously obtained, roared into action after two tugs on the rope. We plugged in the long extension that carried juice from the garage location into the house. Refrigerator and freezer motors purred with pleasure as the juice arrived. A stand lamp chased shadows that eluded the glow of candles and kerosene. We checked the list of appliances that could be run by our 5,000-watt lifesaver.

"Microwave oven?" asked Alice.

"Sure, only takes 600 watts. The freezers take 1,200, refrigerator 500, lamp 100, radio 50. That's 2,450 altogether. No problem."

"We'll have catfish casserole for dinner. I've got a microwave recipe."

Next on the list, with birds and humans handled, were the patient cattle huddled in the lee of the barn a quarter-of-a-mile away. Tree limbs had to be dragged out of driveway and road before the Jeep could slither up to the pasture gate. From there, afoot, I moved toward the herd. Old Twenty-four, the matriarch, crunched toward me, expectantly. A younger cow mooed softly. Their coats were black as anthracite, curly as Caracul.

As I rounded the corner, Lone Valley Paradise, the new bull exited the barn hastily.

As all four feet hit the exterior cement slab, he started to slide like a skier on a slope. He looked puzzled, kept his balance, found somewhat surer footing when he reached the crusted ground. They all watched me and waited. Half-a-bale apiece, nine bales to be thrown down from the haymow, scattered on the ground. It was too slick to carry bales to the round feeders thirty yards away. Water was no problem. The heavy, surefooted animals could pick their way to an open spring at the edge of the lake.

The lake itself would also supply water for washing and flushing at the house. The generator wasn't rigged to run our pump so it would be a bucket by bucket operation for the moment. For drinking water we had the ten or so gallons we had gained just before the lights went out. Ample wood was stacked, under canvas, just beyond the back door. Come ahead, Nineteenth Century, we're ready for you.

Miraculously, the area telephone lines had been placed underground just the past year. So, around ten the next morning, the phone rang.

"Just wanted to check and see if you're O.K." It was George.

"Fine, how about you?"

"No problems."

There were half-a dozen similar calls from up and down the road.

Late in the afternoon the sun came out. Acres of diamonds scintillated around us. We took pictures and knew they would never capture the glitter, sparkle, fairyland beauty of what we saw.

"Happy New Year, Alice."

"Happy New Year, Ken."

"Not a bad place to be, is it?" she asked.

"Not bad at all."

"I can remember when something like this would have had you raving," she reminisced. "You have changed."

"In the city," I speculated, "I would now be bonkers. We'd be waiting for somebody else to fix things."

Out in the garage the new generator kicked over at the first pull of the starter rope and settled into a reassuring hum. For four days it kept the deep freezes frozen, illuminated our evenings, and microwaved our meals. Thanks to a lucky purchase the Nineteenth Century never quite arrived.

Today the tools and toys that augur the high-tech twenty-first are very much with us. Computer, word-processor, calculator, video cassette player, all have moved into our lives. They are nice. Real steps forward, every one, making work easier, leisure more enjoyable.

But, come the unexpected, they won't give you the warm feeling a good wood stove will nor light up your life like a kerosene lamp.

Probably it's perverse, but, in retrospect, I think we got more pleasure out of handling the Big Freeze than some of our friends found in a concurrent Caribbean Cruise, and our photographic record is more dazzling than is theirs.

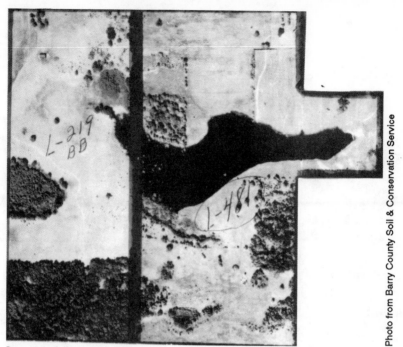

Photo from Barry County Soil & Conservation Service

An aerial map clearly defines the twenty-acre lake, surrounded by swampland, pasture area, woods, fence lines.

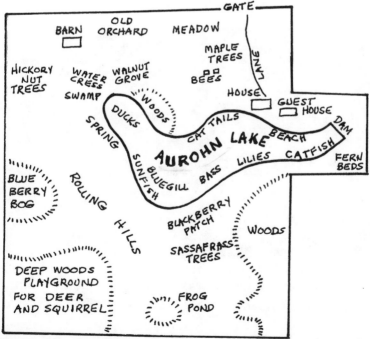

GATE

BARN   OLD ORCHARD   MEADOW

MAPLE TREES

HICKORY NUT TREES   WATER CRESS   WALNUT GROVE   BEES

SWAMP   LANE

HOUSE

WOODS   GUEST HOUSE

SPRING   DUCKS   CAT TAILS   BEACH   DAM

AUROHN LAKE   LILIES   CATFISH

SUNFISH   BLUEGILL   BASS   FERN BEDS

BLUE BERRY BOG   ROLLING HILLS   BLACKBERRY PATCH   WOODS

DEEP WOODS PLAYGROUND FOR DEER AND SQUIRREL   SASSAFRASS TREES   FROG POND

Weekend discoveries led to Alice's own more descriptive map.

To start with, there were glorious fields of Queen Anne's lace, chicory, goldenrod and brush. A second-hand mobile home provided shelter.

On a summer afternoon, when the bluegills were biting, the little lake in Michigan was as far from boardrooms, freeways, frantic deadlines and cocktail parties, as Tahiti or Hawaii.

At the lake, he's a truck driver, tractor operator, fence-mender, fixer, explorer, hunter, fisherman, would-be farmer.

A maker and teacher of advertising, Ken's clients have included Chevrolet, Oldsmobile, Pillsbury, Singapore Tourist Board, Consumers Power, Archway, Upjohn.

Photos by Chuck Fedorowicz

Contentment didn't come with leisure, but, for Alice, with watching a garden produce food for the table, for pantry shelves and freezers. It wouldn't win blue ribbons at the county fair, but, grown organically, it provides bonuses in nutrition and flavor.

Photo by authors

Photo by Chuck Fedorowicz

Ken and Marty's once-a-year calf crop come in early April and is ready for market by November. It's young, organic beef, raised on native grass and mother's milk.

The adventure is endless. Dr. William Batz, naturalist and neighbor, discovered the state's largest Shadbush tree also called Juneberry or Serviceberry just across lake. It was confirmed as U. S.'s largest in 1983, lost title in '87.

Photo by Carl Bennett

107

A Silver Salute from Cooperative Extension Service at Michigan State University recognizes contributions to community through service on Planning and Zoning, Parks and Recreation, Economic Development Commissions.

10

Making It Pay

ALICE:

ONE OF LIFE'S great lessons lies in getting what you want and then finding out it's not exactly what you thought it was. Like a place in the country where we could enjoy our golden years. That's what I certainly wanted. Hand-in-hand my husband and I would stroll the meadows and woodlands and give truth to Browning's lines:

"Grow old along with me,
The best is yet to be."

No longer subject to deadlines and demands, he would mellow, grow sweeter with the years. Together we would learn more about the wild flowers, observe the ways of bird and beast, enjoy the land around us.

Farming was never part of the vision.

Not for me, anyway.

Farming was my father's life, remembered vividly.

Hearing him go downstairs at 4 A.M., in order to get the milking done. Joining him at 6 A.M., to help run our small-town milk route, then getting dropped off at school. Seeing him come in long after dark, bone-weary, after a day of hay making. Watching him and mother go over the books, worried about taxes, land payments. Seeing him go grim when a machine broke down and we didn't have the money for spare parts. Sharing in a family's despair when blackleg threatened the whole milking herd of Holsteins. Wondering when it would rain as corn leaves turned brown, or when the sun would shine as tractors bogged down in mud.

There was no need to relive all of that. Our land, in my mind, was to be enjoyed, not used. Of course it had once been a farm. Rusted, sagging fences marked old fields.

There were stone piles showing where land had been cleared and cultivated. But that was long ago and now brush was marching into the pastures. The weathered, gray barn could stay empty, the fields where Ira's sheep had grazed, lie fallow. The acres could rest from productive labor, just as we would. It was a place for living, not livelihood. The farmer's daughter had never wanted to be a farmer's wife. So I felt a few qualms when Ken informed me that he was getting a new Land Plan.

Once he had asked John Hamp, the local soil conservationist, why the first Plan was so simple. John chuckled and said:

"I figured you for city folks. I didn't think you'd be around for more than a couple of years."

Little did he know.

That original Conservation Plan didn't demand much. A little mowing and brushhogging to keep the land from going completely wild, rye grass and fescue planted to stop erosion, some rows of corn, soybeans and buckwheat grown as food for wild creatures, five hundred Austrian pine trees to beautify and improve some rough hillsides. That was it for the original ninety acres. Now, with the addition of sixty, Ken felt a compulsion to make it all productive.

It was disquieting. I knew, first hand, what it was like to live with a man bent on making the earth yield its bounty. There was something inexorable about the way Ken plunged ahead. He contacted Walt Summers, the new Soil Conservationist for Barry County.

Now it was his turn to walk the place from end-to-end, side-to-side. He noted everything: the Land Capability map drawn up by his predecessor showing romantic names like Parkhill loam, Metea loamy sand, Marlette loam, meaningless to me but important to the plan; the kinds of trees that grew in the woods, oaks and beech, ironwood and tulip, some useful, some not; the contours and water holes, marshes and meadows and hedgerows.

Walt and his wife came to dinner and we talked late about our hopes and dreams. He took more notes. He let it be known that his basic sympathies were with the wilderness, that whatever we did should provide continuing shelter for wildlife, that, ideally, we would effect a compromise between productivity and refuge for the native inhabitants, bird and beast alike. That was fine with us, especially me. After weeks, months of consideration, it came. A blue binder with a completely detailed and coded map and twelve pages, single-spaced, of precisely worded directives. With it a laconic note:

Dear Ken

Attached is your copy of a new plan for your property. I hope you will be able to take a little time out to review it. We will get together sometime soon to discuss it.

Sincerely

Walt Summers

We did. All that remained was to put it into action. That was a dozen years ago and, with slight and recent revisions, the plan has held us to a steep and winding road that has no end. That story belongs to Farmer Ken.

KEN:

It is a paradox, isn't it? Alice, the farm girl, turns out to be a country romantic and city-bred me, the agriculturist.

If memory serves me, it really all started with Kendall, the local auctioneer and a man with a keen eye for gain. During our first year of possession he had given us fifty dollars for the use of fifty acres and had grazed seventeen head of cattle there for six months. The price of cattle was pretty high at the time and I computed the worth of the weight they had put on and decided that beef production had possibilities. The following year Charlie, my neighbor, put fifteen calves to grazing on our pastures, and gradually increased the herd to thirty. My recompense was one whole steer for beef. Now, built into the new Land Plan, was the chance to do it all on my own. The statement is etched in memory: *"These combined pastures will adequately support 35–40 animals."* That was the way to self-sufficiency, solvency, and even modest riches.

Some strange sort of deep-seated, maybe even neurotic, need to be productive had overcome my original motives for the move to the country. That occurred to me often as agriculture became a vocation. Now began the pursuit of the most elusive dollars ever chased.

Item One on the Land Plan: Hayland Planting.

Quote: "In order to prepare these two fields for a hayland seeding they may be planted to corn for two years in order to break up the existing sod." Notice that the directive does not mention rocks. I guess the planners just take them for granted. But the folks who agreed to plow and plant for me didn't:

"Can't take our machinery in there until a lot of the rocks are out," said Dick Havens. He and his wife, Mary, had agreed to plant the corn on shares.

"I'll get right at it," seemed to be the only appropriate reply. I hooked a little wagon intended to haul a recreational vehicle on behind the Jeep truck. Working fast I could fill that wagon up while traversing fifty feet of ground.

How many fifty-foot swaths there are in twenty-one acres is something not computed but it is about a million tons of rocks.

"Why are we doing this?" the complaining back would creak.

"To prepare for profit." the accountant in me replied.

"Ouch," said the back, "Is it worth it?"

"Just pick up the stones and stop thinking," said the accountant, "That's what backs are for."

Corn, that first year, never reached the magic $3.00 per bushel figure that it is supposed to yield in order to pay for chiropractic treatments, a home heat lamp, and tubes of Ben Gay. We sold the grain for what we could get and hoped for better things ahead.

The second year prices were a little better but weather and other things kept us from getting the corn picked before winter's arrival. So, in January and February, on freezing days, I would walk the field with bushel baskets and wrest the ears from stiff stalks and take them to some pigs in which I owned a half-interest. That's called conversion of crops to meat. We eventually sold two pigs and ate one but, all up, I doubt if that paid for the corn seed. The pork was delicious.

The third year arrived and it was time to make hay. But it had become increasingly apparent that the course I had embarked upon was not for solo flying. I needed a partner. The Havens were simply not in a position to do all that had to be done in the next crucial year. Good, old Providence was ready again. About a mile from us, Marty Preston had a dairy farm. He was milking 15 head of Holsteins, managing about 120 acres that provided their feed.

Marty is the prototype small farmer, hard put to stay in business, every cent tied up in needed machinery, seed, fertilizer, chemicals. He's a man of great faith and that's what sustains him through droughts, blizzards, price fluctuations, mastitis, power failures, and pronouncements from Washington about farm policies.

Marty is a country boy. He would rather bow hunt than bar hop, catch fish than make deals, run a trapline than ride a freeway. He literally loves the land and what it offers. So, when I asked him to join me in what he calls the beef cow business, I was hopeful that he would agree. Because it offered a way to earn extra income without the imprisonment of factory or shop, he did. I would furnish land, capital, animals, buildings. His contributions were strength, knowledge and machinery. One-third of whatever we could realize in gross income would be his. We started with a handshake and only when there was real equity in the operation did we draw up some simple papers of agreement.

What was important at first was action. More stone-picking for me, soil samples to be taken in for analysis, a check of the terrain for him, filling in gullies, figuring out how to best plant the steeply sloping hillsides. We would leave an apron of land untouched around the lake to prevent runoff. In early spring the big lime trucks came, balloon tired, and spread a white dusting to enrich the soil. Finally we were ready for fertilizer and seeding, and, in late July, the alfalfa was planted. There was nothing to do now except hope for a wet, mild winter and see what spring would bring. It brought a lovely, delicate pattern of early green in orderly rows and we were on our way.

Those twenty acres, although they still seem to regurgitate stone from somewhere, manage to produce us 1,500 to 2,000 sixty-pound bales of fine hay every summer. It was quite marvelous that first year to stand in the dimness of the seventy-five year old barn, with walls of hay reaching up to the roof, and to simply smell the richness. There's a promise of sustenance there, a preparation for the worst that winter can do, and it comes from the goodness of the land.

Our first animals were a polyglot bunch picked up at farm auctions. Most were Angus, with a few Holsteins to fatten up and sell. Particularly memorable were two Red Polls that started running the minute they exited the cattle truck at our gate. They were supercows. They could clear tall fences at a single bound, outrun fast horses, outlast the most tenacious man.

Like deer, they would skulk in underbrush, hide in swamps. We were finally able to contain the less agile of the pair, but its mate literally went wild. Neighbors would spot it grazing with their herds, or it would turn up, bawling, just outside our fence line. The only way we could recapture that investment was for Marty to take his rifle, stalk Roamin' Red, and bring her back for the deep freeze.

Another vividly remembered escape artist was an old cow that belonged to Charlie. She had borne a number of calves in his barn. When she joined our herd she was simply homesick. Fenced in and frustrated on three sides she figured a simple solution. The fourth side was the lake. So, leaving the rest of the herd watching and astonished, she dived in, swam across and was last seen legging it up the hill toward the barn.

"If she likes it here that much," Charlie said, "we'll just let her stay."

The fences were far from secure in those early years and that added to the exercise and excitement. The phone would ring and a kind local friend would advise us:

"Your cows is out."

Four words that you really hated to hear. Sometimes, when the animals were in the road, you could get close with the Jeep truck and push them back along the roadway. For a while we had an all-terrain vehicle that we employed as an ersatz cow pony careening over hill and dale. Mostly, though it was leg work. Heading them off, turning them, pushing them toward the fence break that was the escape place, hoping they would go back the way they had come. To accelerate the heart rate it beats aerobics, squash, and jogging.

The eventual solution was our own rural electrification program. We threw a charge into every perimeter fence on the place. It handles the cow problem, by and large. Sometimes a fallen branch, driven deer, wind-twisted wire, or inexplicable break shorts the fence. In which case it is best to walk to the barn and switch off the juice before making repairs. Sometimes, to save steps, I've removed a limb without exercising that precaution. Holding down the wire with one hand and lifting the branch with the other is not recommended. It is a way of gaining comprehension of the cow's reluctance to come in contact with the fence. As the power flows through your glove, into your hand and up your arm you know, positively, why they stay about four feet away from the wire.

Once we had reasonably serviceable fencing, an assured supply of hay and a few cattle fattening for the market, it was time for the forward look. What next? The answer was in a classified ad in the local weekly:

FOR SALE: Eight registered Angus cows. Bred.

A phone call, an inspection trip by Marty and me, a check for $6,000 and they were ours. They had neckchains and numbers for identification, and, on their papers they had wonderful names: Black Velvet Uncas, Black Velvet Revolution, Miss Sunshine, Queen Barbara, Karen of Barryville, Favorite Lass, those were some of them. They were tame and gentle and Number 24, Uncas, was as friendly as an oversized pup. As they stepped down from the trailer that brought them they looked around their new digs. They jostled each other, began to move down the hill below the barn. We watched them take their first drink from the lake. In time they were joined by a splendid bull, Evergreen Freestate II, and the families began. Now it was Aurohn Angus Farm, and a new way of life.

Part of it was hot August days lifting bales to the wagon bed, gentling the tractor up a hill while the load rocked precariously, shoving the square bundles off the wagon on to the elevator and into the barn. In winter it could mean plodding through drifts on snowshoes to reach the clustered herd. Roads were closed, Marty couldn't get out, and the animals had to be fed. How grateful they seemed as the bales thudded to the ground, how patient. They waited while you pulled the binder twine loose, lifted the loose hay into the feeders. You looked back as you left and saw them, a black circle, chewing, confident that each day a two-legged friend would show up and provide. Maybe spring is the best time. With April, the new calves begin to arrive, one or two each day. Wet and wobbly, avidly tugging at teats, utterly attached to the mothers who stamp nervously when you approach, and look aggrieved as you insert ear tags in the ears of their bawling offspring.

There are times when cold rain is falling and we want shelter for a calf. Then Marty and I must carry the fifty- or sixty-pound baby up the hill to the barn. What a head-shaking, stamping, defiant creature the mother becomes! One of us must fend her off, while the other carries the young one.

Want excitement to encourage the adrenalin flow? You'll get it when the vet comes and you run the whole herd through the headgate for tagging and checking. Such a bellowing and pushing in the barn. Tell them it's for their own good if you will, but they 'll have none of it and have to be shoved and shouted into the chute.

How much they add to the esthetics of the place on a summer evening at sunset. Gold sky, emerald hillside, onyx cattle set against it. Twenty cows, twenty calves and a lordly bull living here, on our place.

But, the purpose was not the picturesque, but the practical and, eventually, that meant marketing. Like the corn prices, the cattle prices plunged as soon as we began producing.

How could we justify the cost of an addition to the barn, new fencing, supplementary feed? At the prices being paid in the auction ring we couldn't. Again, an answer to the dilemma simply walked into our lives.

Eldon Houghtaling came over to look at our calves, thinking to get one for his grandson's 4-H project. Wanted a crossbred animal, Charolais and Angus and we happened to have one. Turned out he raised purebred Angus, too. Prices were terrible so he had worked out his own business. He found people with home freezers who wanted fine, young beef. Natural stuff, no chemicals, no steroids or fattening with extra grain. Firm, lean stuff. That's what he sold, young beef seven or eight months old, four, maybe five-hundred pounds to the animal. He didn't buy a calf, but he sure left an idea. Marty liked it.

"We'd sell in November," he said, "all except a few heifers we'd keep for replacement. That way we wouldn't be wintering more than twenty. Save a lot of hay and we wouldn't need to use the barn."

We used the reciprocity principle to start our sales effort. Our good friend and long-time accountant said he'd give Aurohn Organic Beef a try. So did our investment counselor. The fact that they lived a hundred and twenty miles away didn't deter us. The trick was to build enough business to make the long haul profitable. Three other friends with families and food lockers came through with orders. That meant a half-ton payload for the pickup truck. We fattened the project by soliciting a few local customers and, presto, we were in the meat business.

If it sounds simple, don't be misled. So many things can happen. Like they did one day in early December when we were getting ready for our last long haul. The weather had turned unseasonably warm, but we figured that by starting early, covering the meat with old quilts and tarpaulins, and hurrying, we could handle the final five deliveries before anything thawed.

We were at the loading platform behind the processing plant at 7:00 A.M. I was lifting the first rather heavy box aboard and there was a ripping sound.

"What's the matter?" Alice asked when she heard my groan.

I knew what had happened. I could feel the draft.

"My pants," I explained. "The seat just ripped out."

She didn't dare laugh. We finished loading as quickly as possible and then detoured back home for a quick change before heading for the city. That used up a precious forty-five minutes as the day began to warm. Then we settled back and headed for the house of our first customer in a posh suburb. We were tooling down a six-lane freeway, just twenty miles from destination, when the engine started to miss. I managed to steer the truck into a restaurant's driveway just as it quit altogether. The restaurant was closed and the sun was high in the heavens as I darted across the wide and busy expanse of concrete in search of a pay phone.

We were members in good standing of the American Automobile Club and their Emergency Service was pledged to get us started or towed. In response to my Mayday call they assured immediate rescue. After waiting an hour I hazarded another dash across the freeway and called again. Unfortunately, all emergency trucks were otherwise occupied but it wouldn't be long. After another half-hour we decided to get at least part of the cargo delivered. Scuttling across the six-lanes again I telephoned Jay Sweeney, our nearest client, and suggested he come to where we were and take his 200 pounds of fine beef. He concurred and was there in a trice. Jay happens to be a curious guy so he sought the cause of our immobility. He even crawled under the truck and tapped the gas tank. It rang hollowly.

"There's your trouble," he said. "It's empty."

Then off he went to get a five gallon can of precious petrol while I explained to Alice that our gasoline tank wouldn't hold its prescribed twenty-gallons since I had dented it badly driving over a log. That was the reason the gas gauge lied. My careful explanation didn't erase a certain glint in her eye.

Thanks to our Samaritan, we were soon on our way again. He promised to call the Triple A and explain that their Emergency Service was no longer necessary. Even with fresh fuel, the truck engine did considerable sputtering and kept us on edge while we delivered to the next three clients. At our final stop I briefed Nick Wyte, another old friend from advertising agency days, as to why we were an hour and a half behind our appointed time. He has mechanical talents, as does his son, and they had the hood up before their meat was in the freezer.

"That engine is really filthy," said father.

"Needs a complete tune-up", declared son.

We concurred and, fortified with one cocktail and some snacks, which included some of Nick's home-made caviar, we headed home. None of the meat had thawed and it was all properly ensconced in freezer chests in the city and three suburbs.

As we reached the half-way point on the way home, truck empty, but wallet fattened with five substantial checks, we indulged ourselves. There's a fancy restaurant just off the highway, and despite our worse-for-the-wear appearance we stopped and had a wonderful dinner. I was glad I had changed my pants.

The next day I took the truck in for points, plugs and a general overhaul.

Our beef business is not exactly a living, but it almost pays the property taxes. What otherwise would be brushland is pasture and hayfield. We both have gotten a lot of exercise. And those black cattle do look beautiful against the emerald hills.

Fortune continues to favor us. With the keen and continuing interest in chemical-free foods, our beef is more attractive to more people than ever before. A Co-op food store in Grand Rapids now retails Aurohn Angus Beef, and Mike Bowering, the manager says the demand is growing. Our delivery problems are simpler, now. Alice can load a couple of forty pound boxes into the back of the station wagon and simply deliver them to the store! She should have the last word on the subject of agriculture.

ALICE:

Little did I know that twenty years after I discovered Paradise, it would turn into a farm. Had I but known, I'd have made sure that the land area involved was no bigger than the water area. But here I am, back to girlhood on the farm. Making phone calls to customers, lining up the butcher, concerned with giving our clients everything they ordered and we promised. Listening to Ken and Marty speculate on the possibility of rain to bring on the hay, or a dry spell so they can harvest it. Running into town to pick up a patched tractor tire. Making calls to the veterinary.

I thought all those hard realities of farm life had been happily exchanged for the complexities of city life. Not that I was ever totally comfortable in that environment, but the advertising business did seem preferable to the farming business in terms of requirements and rewards.

It was a little shocking to see Ken metamorphose from

fisherman to farmer. Instead of grumping about the failure of his favorite lure, now he frets about early frost and the high cost of fertilizer. He'd said he wanted to fish and loaf, that he didn't even want a lawnmower on the place. Now we've got two tractors and it takes five hours to cut the grass. Well, it's not what we came for, but it does add drama to our lives.

I have a new appreciation for those nineteenth century pastoral pictures, the ones that show lasses in dirndls out in the wheat fields, bringing in the sheaves. They're not doing it for fun and fresh air. Up ahead, somewhere, the old man is swinging his scythe and yelling: "Hurry up! It looks like rain."

Sometimes, when the gods want a good laugh, they answer your prayers!

11

The
Woods

KEN:

THERE WAS a time in our lives when we were good church members. Every Sabbath morning we deposited our kids in their Sunday School classes, then went off to teach. Alice, using flannel boards and sandboxes, told toddlers about the opening of the Red Sea, Daniel in the Lion's Den, Samson and the Philistines, David and Goliath and other exciting tales from the Old Testament. I matched wits with high-school seniors who found a good deal of the Old Testament and much of the New subject to question, and who detected certain discrepancies in the professed theology of their society and the way that society behaved. Rationalizing Christianity for them was hard work. The rest of those long-ago mornings was devoted to Church, which our son and daughter found less than fascinating, and, finally, as a reward, Sunday Brunch at a restaurant nearby. That was the pattern until the fledglings flew and we were alone in the nest, a time that, happily, coincided with the beginning of our new life at the lake.

The hours there were just too precious to be interrupted by a

122

drive into town, by the constrictions of buttoned collar and up-tight tie, makeup and hose, and hours in a closed sanctuary, how-ever beautiful.

So, instead, on Sunday mornings, our way of worship became a walk in the woods. Sometimes, I still have qualms of conscience over our retreat from organized religion. It's assuaged somewhat by fairly regular attendance at Dr. Robert Schuller's television tabernacle. His messages about possibility thinking seem so ap-propriate just before we set out seedlings in heavy clay.

But, on many Sundays, the only choir we'll hear is the sough of wind in burly beeches and high oaks, the frogs' chant in the swamp. Our only connection with Heaven is the slanting light that streams downward through soaring trees, and our prayers are uttered silently as we follow an old lumbering trail through our forest.

According to the land plan this Big Woods is just under 18 acres. To any timber baron that hardly justifies the appellation "big." But stand in the middle of it, under a black walnut whose straight trunk soars sixty feet above you, make your way around a maze of storm-toppled popples, watch a family of squirrels ca-vort around an old wolf beech tree that canopies a circle thirty feet in diameter, and it seems plenty large enough. It is a king-dom unto itself, entirely unrelated to pasture and hayfield. It's still the wild place.

Walk quietly in from the edge. Find a tree to lean against and sit down. Don't move. At first, on a day when the winds are still, you'll be impressed by the silence. Your incursion quiets all the inhabitants. Give it five or ten minutes. Then the chipmunks chirp and soon are on the move. They'll eye you, motionless, and if you remain that way they are liable to run right across your shoe. Next, from a tree top, hear the sassy bark of a fox squirrel as he decides all is well. Look up and you'll see his orange tail jerking in time to his discourse. Some yards away there's a reply and a dialogue ensues.

Sit still. There, not thirty yards away, comes a doe and a fawn. Every move is tenative. She nibbles at some brush, looks up, cocks her ears, turns her nostrils to and fro, nibbles again, steps daintily ahead. The fawn imitates her. Fortunately the wind is in your favor, she never catches your scent and they pass within fifteen feet of your vantage point.

Get up noisily and watch the action. Straight up go the tails, white flags of warning. Two tremendous bounds and the doe is gone, the fawn trying to keep up. The squirrel zips around the tree and out of sight, the chipmunks pop down holes, under logs, and are still.

Walk fifty yards and do it over again, wait a long time. Once a wary fox stole by within a stone's throw. Another time we saw a a partridge drumming on a log. There was an evening when a family of coons arose from their beds deep in a den tree. They trooped out, four of them, and each sat on a different limb. They yawned and stretched, rubbed their eyes, for all the world like a suburban foursome getting ready to face the day. One by one they came down the trunk and, in file, headed for the lake's edge, probably with succulent crawfish in mind to serve as their nocturnal breakfast.

The woods are for hunting, too. In the early fall a few bushytails are picked off and once the guns have spoken how silent the other squirrels stay, how quickly they learn to head for den trees when there is man movement on the ground. It's the same with the deer during the last weeks of November. They move out of the woods and into the densest swamps, stay there until nightfall, then come out to browse and drink. Only by wearing hipboots and kicking through the swamps can you move them during hunting hours. Once the season is past, they return to the woods and move on their accustomed trails. The woods are and will be the wild place, but, like the rest of the land, they too have been cultivated.

Walt Summers, who did the Land Plan, is a graduate forester and he had a lot to say about Woodland Improvement. Like:

"The quality and condition of the timber will be enhanced by a program of Timber Stand Improvement (TSI). Undesirable plant species such as wildgrape vines, blue beech, ironwood, sassafras and the larger 'wolf' beech trees will be discriminated against by cutting. Very poorly formed and misshapen trees will also be cut where their removal would be of benefit to neighboring superior trees."

He didn't just write about it. He walked us through the timber and showed us. This noble oak had many good years ahead of it. That one, which looked almost identical, should be sold and removed. Telltale holes and dead branches indicated that it was hollow inside and would fall to wind and weather before too long. Cut now it could yield some good saw logs. Wait and it would be worthless. The variety of species that he pointed out was amazing. He drew a map and indicated where each grew. On the steep slopes and in the wet bottom lands there were white oaks, shagbark and bitternut hickories, American beech, black cherry, basswood and aspen. On the flatter land was northern red oak and some valiant elm attempting a comeback after the ravages of the Dutch elm disease. There was aspen, a few maples.

"Looks like there was selective cutting when maples were bringing premium prices," Walt explained. "That happens. A lot of folks are selling off black walnuts as veneer logs right now because that's what the market wants."

He pointed out some beautiful tulip poplars, sometimes called whitewoods and told us to watch for their flowering in the spring.

"If you do any cutting," he suggested, "leave the black walnut and tulips. Give them a chance to reseed."

On the first measure to be taken he was quite insistent.

"Get a fence up and keep the livestock out." He told us why.

"There are generations of trees missing, no small ones coming on. Try to find any sizeable saplings and all you see is ironwood, dogwood, some witch hazel. This was all grazed by sheep for years and the good young stuff couldn't get started."

It was true. Ira Tobias's hungry ewes had eaten the acorns, hickory and walnuts, the butternuts, the flavorful black cherry saplings and tulip tree shoots and had, thereby, created a forest without a future. In the meantime the subtle seeds of decay were affecting the mature trees. Lightning opened wounds that never really healed, frost split bark and opened the way for rot, giant oaks developed circulatory problems. A ruthless cycle of dying oldsters and few replacements would spell eventual doom for the hardwood forest. What had looked to us like a lovely, everlasting forest was, to the educated eyes of a forester, a huge organism to be cared for, and kept in balance.

The fence was the first order of business that spring. Another paragraph from the Land Plan gave us the next order.

"The mature timber, predominantly red and black oak, beech and black cherry will be harvested using a selection cut method. The timber will be sold on contract, by bid, to a commercial timber firm. Roads, skidding trails and yarding areas will be designated in advance of the sale. Care will be taken to minimize damage to the residual stand and to prevent fire."

Thanks to Walt's timber cruise and advice, we were ready to deal with the other side of the coin, the commercial timber people. What they are looking for is maximum production, the largest number of usable saw logs from the smallest possible area.

Logging is still a risky business, requiring skilled people and heavy machinery. Weather can slow the operations down and the requirements of the landowner are inhibiting to speed. So, before the dozers and skidders and chainsaws move in, it's important to have clear understandings and a written contract.

As Walt had suggested, we walked the ground with timber scouts from three different companies, discussed our objectives, got bids from each and, based on those bids, arrived at an agreement with Jerry Tomandl whose outfit has the reassuring name of Quality Lumber.

Jerry marked trees in two ways. With an orange circle he designated those that had real value to the lumber company, oaks, ash, cherry, primarily. They were mature trees, about to "go backwards" as growth gave way to decay. With an orange "X" he marked the less valuable trees that were to be removed for purposes of reforestation. These beeches and aspens had minimum commercial value but he would take them as part of the deal. Of the ninety-nine trees marked, two-thirds were desireable hardwoods, one-third were marginal from Jerry's point of view but would improve the woods from mine.

Once the marking was completed, Walt Summers came out took a look and gave the project his blessing. He also suggested the provisions for a contract to be signed before a single tree was felled. Skidding would be along existing trails, trees to be bucked into eight foot lengths at the stump to prevent damage to other, standing trees as logs were dragged out, trails to be leveled at the end of the operation, brush to be stacked, and a security bond of $300 to be posted to cover possible damage to stand and land during the logging operation. These were matters the neophyte landowner would never have considered without expert advice.

Everything was ready, papers all signed, work to start within two weeks. It had been a cold winter, ground frozen hard, ideal conditions. Two hours after the signing it started to snow. Ankle deep, knee deep, hip deep it piled up, snowshoes were needed to even get to the woods. It was a reprieve for the marked trees and meant a six week wait until an early thaw cleared the way for work.

The day came soon enough when the once silent forest became a place of controlled bedlam. Chain saws whined, the skidder roared, the giants groaned and creaked and crashed to the ground. It was hard to listen to the death of the ancients; and we tried to think of it as surgery, necessary to the long term health of the whole woods.

The success of the operation depended on the skill of the practitioners, Roger, the sawyer, and Pat, who piloted the powerful skidder. To watch Roger notch, saw and fell one of the big red oaks, placing it so that its tons of tumbling weight caused minimal damage to other trees, was to watch a kind of artistry. Pat, in turn, manuevered his skidder and its load of logs along the narrow trail that had been opened, careful not to scrape the trees still standing.

It was ten months after his initial cruise of the timber when

Walt came back to see what had resulted. The last of the logs had been dragged into the pasture where they could be loaded onto trucks and hauled away to the mill. The woods were quiet on this day in mid-March, the ground softening under the melting snow. Even with the massive tree tops recumbent on the ground, still to be cut and cleared, it was apparent that the forest floor had been opened up to the sun and that seedlings would have a long-delayed chance to grow and prosper. Spring rains would fill in the remaining ruts caused by the machinery. Cordwood cutting over the summer would eliminate the rubble and give us fuel for stove and fireplace for the next three or four years.

"That one was ready to go." Walt pointed to stump that was nearly thirty inches across. The center was badly rotted. More than half of the trees cut had obvious signs of disease, detected originally, by the practiced eyes of Walt or Jerry, and by tapping trunks with a wooden mallet.

The first big step in our timber stand improvement program had been taken at a propitious time. A diminished national oil supply sent fuel costs soaring, and friends and neighbors were switching from oil and electric heat to wood furnaces and stoves. In our own case the room-by-room electric heat that had seemed eminently practical and affordable was now prohibitively expensive. We switched from the decorative but inefficient Franklin stove we had originally installed, to an airtight, highly utilitarian Defiant from the fledgling Vermont Castings Company. Cordwood became our mainstay for keeping cozy.

Again, chainsaws sounded harshly in the forest. We worked out plans for cutting on shares with half-a-dozen families; and pickup trucks shuttled in and out along the healed logging trails as tops and branches were converted into stove-sized hunks. Behind our garage a head-high stack reached twenty-by-twenty foot proportions as the pickups delivered our share and I tried to keep it orderly. One neighbor, Howard Hostetler, had a great device he pulled behind his tractor. It was an old manure spreader that he had converted into a log hauler. A small engine activated its chain drive and it automatically unloaded its cargo.

Some of the delivered wood was far too fat to fit the stove so sledge and wedges and log-splitters got added to our tool supply and I learned the satisfaction of a well-placed whack that could cleave a log in two. My neighbor has a nifty power splitter, and as time goes by it looks more and more attractive. Before too long there may be another gasoline engine for me to fret over but my back will get a rest.

Six years after that commercial cutting, and as part of a continuing program encouraged by Area Forester, Fred Wuerthle, I had the woods looked at again. Steve Kalisz, a professional Forestry Consultant, came out to determine what had to be done to qualify the forest as a properly improved tree stand. In addition to eliminating wild grapevines and brush he recommended that nearly three hundred trees of varying sizes be eliminated in order to provide proper growing room for the valuable hardwood seedlings that were emerging since the area had been fenced. Ironwoods and beeches, popples, deformed or dead trees, all were to be harvested. They would supply another generation of fuel for our place and others. Properly managed, there will always be more where that came from, an inexhaustible, self-regenerating supply.

Actually, if we took all available firewood just from along our fencelines each year, it would almost suffice to get us through the winters. Four or five times a century there can be a harvest of giants, too, to augment the income produced by the land.

In one small area, just north of a small swamp, there are a score of young black walnut trees. The timber stand improvement program called for them to be pruned of all branches up to seventeen feet. Thus the trunks can grow straight and tall.

There's a directive, too, for keeping them clear of the Virginia creeper vines that seem to have an affinity for walnut trees and that can choke the life right out of them. Properly cared for and guarded, says the forester, those trees can put two grandchildren through college. They are, indeed, a crop that in the fullness of time can be harvested.

That this is really another kind of farming is attested to by an

organization called the American Tree Farm System. This fra-
ternity of forest owners sets fairly stringent standards, and you
don't get to be a member without abiding by them. Regular
inspections of members' woodlots are made and the inspector, in
our case, is Fred Wuerthle. Not long ago Fred called and invited
me, rather insistently, to the annual dinner of the Soil and Water
Conservation District. It was held in a church hall not far away.
The dinner, prepared by the ladies of the church, was excep-
tional. We saw quite a few people we knew and enjoyed talking
with them. An excellent speaker covered the subject of no-till
farming, a fascinating concept that might, eventually, be useful to
us. After all this Fred Wuerthle stood up and called upon me to
step forward. I have a picture of the occasion. He's handing me a
large rectangular, green and white sign that declares me a member of the Tree Farm system. I'm positively beaming. There's a
small diploma-like certificate that goes with it. Here's what it
says:

> This certifies that the Forest Lands of Mr. and Mrs.
> Kensinger Jones are being managed in a manner that as-
> sures continuous production of commercial forest crops
> in accordance with scientific forest management prac-
> tices approved by the state Tree Farm committee and
> the American Forest Institute.
>
> In recognition thereof, these lands are designated a
> TREE FARM and will remain as such as long as the
> owner and his heirs comply with the approved forest
> management standards.

An honor, it is and a responsibility, too, for me and my heirs.
Fred certainly takes it seriously. He comes out and looks around
and sometimes I get letters like:

"When I was walking over your woodlot I noticed some aspen and beech that have yellow paint marks that have not been
cut or girdled yet. Would you please take care of these trees."

I will.

There is one force at work that pays no attention to the Tree Farm System's standards. The old harridan, Mother Nature, sets her own rules. Right after we took out the ninety-nine big ones she launched a small tornado right down the middle of the forest. The trees we had removed just opened the way for her to slam over some smaller timber, making the clearings bigger. Then she lifted her skirts, flew over the pasture, and dipped down to uproot a beautiful, gnarled, very old apple tree. Then she was gone.

When it comes to thinning, pruning and trimming she has another ruthless method called ICE STORM.

After the most recent one Alice and I walked one part of the woods. An old maple den tree had been halved by the weight of ice, our national champion shadbush had lost twenty feet from its top, a forty foot cherry was uprooted. Encrusted ropes of grapevines had dragged down big branches from white oaks, cedars had bent until they cracked. Mother Nature can make firewood, too, and in her own, rough way she cares for her forests. Now, however, we don't just let things lie.

Tree surgeons came and cared for what was then the country's largest shadbush, trimmed away what was torn, covering scars, putting metal caps over broken trunks, to keep the moisture out. Champions deserve the best.

Nor could we let the old beldame have the last word with fourteen big trees she had toppled through weight and wind. Marty went in with tractor, winch and chain and extricated the massive trunks from the woods, stacked them in the pasture. Eventually a buyer came and what might have been left to rot on the forest floor brought us eight hundred dollars. We had passed the plate, taken up the collection. It would help to pay for the consulting foresters, labor, fencing, chain saw maintenance, and new seedlings that it takes to maintain our cathedral properly.

If we were still in town, church, for me, would be necessary. It was part of my childhood, part of my responsibility to my children, part of an unwritten contract with the community. Alice never felt that way, because, on a dairy farm, Sunday morning was the same as the other six and chores came first. Church was for special days, Easter and Christmas, weddings and funerals. Contact with the divine was May in an apple orchard, all trees adoring with their blossoms, or looking out a bedroom window into a Baltimore oriole's nest.

Now, God willing, through Daily Grace, and a few good works, we'll find our way Home, through the forest.

One act of adoration, this spring, was the planting of three American chestnut seedlings. This marvelous tree was decimated, brought to the edge of extinction by a blight in the early twentieth century.

Now, a few survivors have been found and there's a chance of bringing the species back. That's resurrection for you.

12

Trees

ALICE:

WHERE KEN sees forests, I see trees. I've been in love with them ever since discovering, at five, that I could climb an old short-trunked, big-limbed catalpa tree not far from our front door. My mother allowed me the delusion that the thick branches and big leaves hid me from the world, including her. It followed, therefore, that trees were good friends.

So, naturally, from the start, I felt that we needed trees. There should be some near the house, which there weren't. As for the lake, well, a man-made lake looks just like a man-made lake until trees edge the bank. They provide cover for wild things to slip to the edge and drink without fear of detection. Surely our near neighbors were entitled to that much.

Ken was of a different opinion. Trees would make bank fishing very frustrating, and what was this whole effort really about, anyway? It was fishing, that's what. Not altogether stifled, I still dreamed of tree-lined banks, shadows on the water, singing birds perched on branches and reflected in the shimmering surface.

In the first rough clean-up of our proposed building area, it was painful to see little maple, ash and elm seedlings destroyed.

A better answer occurred to me. Move them! Right to the edge of the lake. Ken would think that our tree lined banks were Mother Nature's doing. A surreptitious tree planting drive began. The next two years saw dozens of little trees being rowed to likely spots where I'd happily launch them on a new life.

Of course any lake needs weeping willows and I found some, on sale, during my very first trip to the grocery store in Hastings. It seemed a good omen so I bought and promptly planted them. They graced the immediate waterfront and had been accepted by Ken, albeit not enthusiastically. They flourished. Branches began to droop over the water like they do in Oriental paintings. There was such an abundance of them. Aha! A new source! I began trimming ends and sticking cuttings into banks. Willow and water were synonymous. *They* surely would do well.

It was with a growing sense of frustration that I watched the willow project. Coming, as I did, from a long line of farmers, and an immediate family of green thumbs, it seemed unfair that fate had cruelly cursed me with a brown one. Each spring a blight apparently affected all the little seedlings so optimistically transplanted the year before. They were simply gone.

So it was with a "well, let's give it another try" that late one fall I moved a five-foot, slender, rooted willow wand to a spot by the cove on the west side of our house.

Before the next spring rolled around we were gone. An overseas assignment found us on the other side of the world. In spite of comforting reports from friends, relatives and neighbors that the house stood, the land greened and flourished, fish obligingly grabbed at worms on hooks, I fretted. What about my willow tree?

Ten months later we took a vacation from the heat of Australia in December. We came home to Michigan's ice and snow and cold, and, to me, it felt wonderful.

One morning I was reveling in the beautiful, white world framed by the window. A little while earlier the silence had been broken by Marty Preston clanking to the lake with his muskrat traps. This yearly trapping effort of his kept to a minimum the damage done by burrowing rodents, to the dam and banks. A trap set under water at a stragetic spot, and held in place by a chain fastened to a stick driven into the mud, quickly drowned the rat. The sale of the furs gave Marty a welcome bit of extra income. It was an all-around satisfactory arrangement.

Binoculars in hand, I observed the trapper's progress along the lake shore. The first joyful change I noticed was on the far side of the cove to the west. A tree had grown. Granted, it was still a slender wand; but the five foot willow was now eight feet tall with far more little branches, observable even in it's denuded winter state. Though they were still pencil thin, my excited imagination clothed them with a profusion of yellowish green leaves capped with happy birds (preferably blue birds).

Completing the picture, half-imagined, half-real was Marty, just coming into view. Against the white, snow-smoothed world, his old red hunting jacket made an exclamation point on a frozen page. To the east lay the dam. The sun was rising above the tops of the trees that grew beyond it. A hawk sailed in the thermal drafts, hoping for an unwary mouse to break out of one of its tunnels in the frozen grasses. To the south a movement in the trees on the hill might have been a deer. Swinging my glasses back to the cove I saw the red exclamation point become a comma as Marty knelt at the lake's edge, setting another trap.

With a smile, I looked for the willow. *It was gone!* I was paralyzed with disbelief. Then, like a tide, revelation swept over me. A brown thumb was *not* the reason for the continuing barren edges of the lake. It was Marty's innocent need for stakes for his traps. Over the years he had cut my saplings as fast as they grew to sufficient size!

He was dumfounded and contrite when I told him why I now wanted him to move twenty feet back from the water's edge before he ever cut another stake.

The whole planting episode ended when we opened the land across the lake to the cattle. Now they graze and trample right up to the water's edge. There is, miraculously, still one weeping willow on the far shore. Somehow it struggled back, survived and grew. But, by and large, Ken is never frustrated by graceful trees that might catch a fly line when he fishes the far bank.

He wasn't as arboreally inclined as I when it came to the rest of the place, either. I felt that our house looked stark and naked sitting on the cleared hillside. We both knew it needed plantings but disagreed heatedly on the kind. I wanted *trees* arching, graceful shade trees. Ken wanted freedom from *leaves*, maybe just a few pines. I wanted ornamental plantings. Ken wanted easy mowing. Fortunately we heard about Jack McCormick, then our area's leading landscaper. He would be objective, and certainly less costly than divorce. He came, saw, designed and did good things.

When Jack finished there were about a dozen trees around the house, placed so prevailing winds would blow most of the leaves to the back forty.

He had found maples and ashes in our distant woods and transplanted twelve foot saplings by easing them out of the ground and onto the bucket of his front end loader. Then he hauled and dropped them into holes already prepared in the locations he'd chosen. Big balls of dirt protected the roots and we didn't lose one of them. There were also two dogwoods and a red bud by the house and a pair of transplanted tamaracks above the septic tank field. Another dozen pines we'd planted four years earlier, near the dam, prospered and gave us year around greenness on the hillside.

The plantings close around the house walls were of ground ivy, rhododendron and creeping juniper. Under them a thick plastic cover and several inches of gleaming white gravel took care of the weed problem.

To the delight of both of us, there were also rocks. Big rocks, pretty rocks, interestingly shaped rocks, all placed to the best advantage among the plantings. These, too, Jack found on Aurohn acres. Railroad ties made sturdy steps, and iron lamps illuminated it all at night. I had my trees and then some. In the ensuing years we've done more planting of our own.

There are the twin maples planted by my brother-in-law,

Buck, and his sons when he and Ken celebrated their twin fiftieth birthday.

There's a locust, too, with its own history.

Shortly after becoming landowners, we had moved to an apartment in downtown Chicago. Hardy, smog-resistant locust trees there earned my admiration and gratitude.

Our leash-led little dog found, at the base of them, her personal and private turf each day. Her lengthy investigation of said turf gave me the opportunity to observe the tree's astonishing long flat seed pods in the fall. Seed! Why not have these lacy leafed lovelies at Aurohn Lake? If they could grow between the cracks of cement in the inhospitable city, think how they would flourish in pure fresh country air! Matching action to thought, I busily collected and husked the seeds out of the big pods. Into the window in the apartment kitchen went trays holding styrofoam cups filled with peat. A locust seed or two was deposited in each. They sprouted, weakly, and were hastily transferred to the country. The slender saplings didn't make much of an impact then. Now, the one survivor is nearly thirty feet tall. It would be considerably more than that if Charlie Tobias's cows hadn't pruned it once, when they broke out of their pasture and found greener fields on our lawn.

There's an apple tree, too, tiny when planted. It gave us two bushels of apples last year. The rest of our projected orchard hasn't done so well. Hard winters and hungry deer and rabbits have taken their toll, as have too-sporadic spraying and plain neglect.

But, there's hope. We've mulched around the fruit trees, mowed between rows. Now we wrap the trunks with wire and mesh cloth. Someone told us that soap slivers repel winter browsers, so we hang the branches with the remains of bars of Dial, Ivory, or whatever. Lately, we've been rewarded with a dozen plums, three pears, and a few peach blossoms.

Maybe our wild, untended orchard has spoiled us. Up near the barn there's one old apple tree that bears bushels of fruit and a few gnarled companions in various stages of decay. The first spring or two Ken said, "I really must spray the fruit trees this year." But the sprayer and the bottles of spray were still in the shed when picking time came. To make anything out of insect-bitten fruit is a big waste of time and I resorted to patronizing a commercial "Pick-UR-Own" apple orchard nearby.

Then, one day, Ken bounced in from the back forty after a fence mending effort with lovely, perfect, and delicious, apples rolling around in the bed of the truck. He'd found our first wild apple tree. Since then, on the hundred and fifty acres, we've discovered fifteen or twenty such trees. No two of them are alike in size, age, or type. The fruits are all different. There are big apples, little ones; red, white, pink, yellow and green ones; hard and soft ones; sweet and sour ones; early and late ones; good and bad ones. But the majority are comparatively free of blemishes. The two or three bushels we pick barely make a dent in the crop, most years, so the cattle, the deer and other wild things continue to keep the brush and grass trampled down around the bases of their favorite trees year after year.

Another fruit tree is the mulberry. Two of them are growing in what was once the dooryard of a long-vanished farm house. A cellar of huge cut stones marks the location of the homestead, and the trees are located just far enough away to suggest the possibility of a one-time chicken yard.

Mulberries were often planted as corner posts for chicken or pig pens, not only for shade, but to provide a tasty addition to the diets of hungry farm creatures. Now, with no competition, the birds and wild animals get it all. (We found an opossum asleep on a limb one day during the heavy bearing season. He'd obviously eaten his fill and was sleeping it off until he became hungry again.)

Ken was jubilant when he first found the mulberry tree and tasted the ripe fruit. It was just the sweet flavor he remembered from when, as a child in St. Louis, he raided a neighbor's tree each summer. With his usual enthusiasm he said,

"I bet they would make a marvelous pie. How about it?"

With far less enthusiasm I said,

"But look at these things! They're so soft they'll squish to pulp just in the picking."

"Oh, well, if that's the only problem, I'll do the picking . . . unsquished, and you can do the pie," was his rejoinder.

Confident that the matter was taken care of to *my* satisfaction, I went about my business. Later Ken took off in the direction of the mulberry tree, bucket in hand, and I thought, "Ha! He'll be back in an hour empty handed and in a less than happy mood."

Wrong. He was gone less than a half hour and was back with half a bucketful, looking smug. True, the berries were mixed with twigs and leaves, but they weren't squished. His method?

He'd taken a large square of plastic, laid it on the thick grass under the tree, and shaken the limbs. Now I was stuck with the job of making a pie. This all happened one evening, so pie making was deferred till the next day.

I awakened early and decided to do the baking before breakfast. Taking the bucket and a pan out on the porch so I could enjoy the morning, I started to work. Picking out a plump, purplish-black fruit, I inspected it. Sticking from deep within its juicy center was a slender green stem. I pulled. The berry squished. Now what? Well, if Ken could be ingenious, so could I. Out came the scissors. Holding it carefully, I snipped off the stem closely, the next, and the next. The long quiet kept Ken in bed till midmorning. When he did appear, rested and cheerful, he said,

"Wow, what's making that delicious smell?"

Pointing to the pie sitting on the kitchen counter, bubbling hot, brown, with red juices oozing out of the slits on the top, I said:

"There it is. Your first and last mulberry pie."

The possums, woodchucks, coons and squirrels can have the mulberry trees. I'll settle for my close-to-home companions; the huge horse chestnut at the top of the hill that produces shiny, brown buckeyes, the twin maple sentries beside the driveway, the towering blue spruce in front of the house, the red bud and dogwoods and flowering crabs that sing springtime every year. Ken loves them all as much as I do and mows around them cheerfully.

There are two other very important young trees not far from the front door. One was badly hurt by the last ice storm. The other withstood it nicely and is doing well. Each spring it produces magnificently scented blossoms. Each fall the long seed pods called lady cigars hang from the branches. They are catalpas. Soon my grandaughter, Keeley, if she so wishes, can climb up in the branches and hide from the world.

Then she'll know, too, that trees are good friends.

13

Growing Things

KEN:

WHEREVER we have lived—Missouri, Illinois, Australia, Michigan—we've grown things. The bigger the lot, the bigger the garden. With the purchase of land measured by acres rather than feet, the possibilities seemed boundless. Until the Revelation! With the new possibilities came new problems. Alice's first efforts at improving the lake property ended in tears. She remembers.

ALICE:

The first thaw came just a month after we bought the place. It seemed the perfect time to start beautifying our homestead. For that purpose my sister had donated a great number of her excess daffodil bulbs. They were exactly the excuse I needed for making the two-hour drive from the city to the lake. Anticipation seems to shorten travel time. The walk from the county road across the spongy thawed field, carrying shovel and bulbs, felt good. It was with real pleasure that I set my foot on the back of the shovel to make the first hole. In my mind's eye I could already see the big yellow blooms dressing up the front of the little fishing shack. I thrust with arms, I pushed with foot. The shovel cut into the surface and stopped. Thrusting harder and stomping with vigor, I managed to sink the sharp-edged blade down six inches. Thinking that perhaps a buried rock was the problem, my mind said:

"Move over a little."

My arms tried to obey instructions, and tried again. Wrestling with determination, the body retrieved the shovel from the ground, almost.

Finally, it came out with a "plop," and hanging tenaciously to the shiny surface was a great blob of sticky clay. Continued efforts produced similar results. I wept, recalling vividly my father's 360 acres of friable Pennsylvania soil. However, tears and all, the bulbs were "planted," finally. They were shoved into what cracks the shovel could make and then they were stomped on. (Amazingly, they did grow, and bloom, and multiply!)

Tentative tests in other areas around the "home site" revealed nothing but the same sticky gumbo that, when exposed to air, turned to solid concrete. Dreams of gardening vanished, though we still read with longing all the successful growing ventures written about in the monthly *Organic Gardening* magazine. If the Sears Roebuck catalog was my childhood "wish book," *Organic Gardening* was my adult one. It kept me dreaming and, a few months later it set me doing, again.

Through the questionable generosity of a good friend we had acquired a trio of Muscovy ducks and the flock had grown to nine. The old shack had been converted to a duck house with a pen and, by spring, a considerable quantity of duck-produced fertilizer had accumulated. It was mentioned, by name, in an O.G. suggestion for an experimental potato patch.

This could be the answer! After coaxing bales of rotting hay from Charlie ("Whatever good is that stuff to anybody!"), I broke them into eight-inch thick layers. These were placed as a large, heavy blanket over seed potatoes we lay, correctly spaced, on the ground just north of the shed.

On top of that went the accumulation off the duck house floor. Voila!! Our first garden. That fall we proudly delivered to the family expert on such matters, my father, several potatoes that he pronounced the biggest he'd ever seen.

Gardening was possible.

The next year, neighbor Dick Secord came up the road with his small tractor and plow to turn over the spot where the potato crop had flourished. In went lettuce, radishes, carrots, cucumbers, tomatoes, peppers, and dill. They flourished, more or less. The first thing to mature were the radishes. Lovely big green tops indicated lovely juicy roots. Then we pulled them. What came out were skinny, tough and twisted things. The little bit of straw mulch from the year previous had not loosened the soil sufficiently. Things growing downward had to fight and push against the clay's solidity for survival. Tender and juicy they were not. Tough and strong and inedible they were. Carrots suffered the same fate. Lesson learned . . . no root vegetables unless it be potatoes under a blanket of straw.

But the taste of fresh lettuce, which had thrived, a juicy bite of a ripe tomato, gave birth to ambition. There was hope for all kinds of goodies. So the 12 × 12 foot garden next became a strawberry bed, thanks to our friend and neighbor, Donna. Her donation of strawberry plants that wouldn't fit in her garden pre-empted available space. Next year's vegetables would go elsewhere.

We looked around. We had grown a successful stand of field corn on one side of the fence. Couldn't we grow veggies on the other?

A spot between the fence and lake near the dock and swimming area seemed a perfect location. It was big enough for the sweet corn Ken wanted to plant, and the garden I dreamed about, but was the soil workable?

An article in a January issue of the O.G. magazine seemed to answer that question. It described the miracles wrought by the

TROY-BILT Roto Tiller. Fantastic!! Pictures showed an 80-year-old woman tilling under a thick weed growth between luxuriant rows of vegetables. She was only using one hand on the tiller, the showoff!

We promptly placed an order and were assured by the manufacturer that it would be delivered before spring.

Marty was already plowing his fields for corn when our little work horse arrived. Perfect timing. Ken jubilantly read instructions, filled the gas tank and the oil resevoir, installed the battery, pressed the starter. The engine purred. He shifted into gear . . . and suddenly raced off through the garden hanging on to the tiller bars. The hard clay resisted the tines and they simply propelled the whole apparatus across the surface. Ken put the machine into neutral, replotted his course, dropped the blades deeper and put it into gear again with a little less throttle. It took off, but not so enthusiastically. The tines bit into the ground; the machine slowed. Ken opened the throttle and the tines dug in.

One length of the garden was traversed with Ken being alternately pulled, stumbling, over great clay clods, or pushing the tiller when it slowed. Coming to the end of the row he threw it into neutral and wrestled the machine around to repeat the process. Then he glanced down. The tines had disappeared. In their place was a huge ball of clay. With a stick and a great deal of effort and angry noises, Ken cleared the tines of the goo. He set the throttle and at a gentle pace, walked behind it to the shed.

Marty could plow on one side of the fence with his big equipment, but on our side of the fence the TROY-BILT needed *exact* moisture conditions for easy tilling. Those conditions prevail about twenty days a year. That's enough.

Our little motorized horse is still serving us well, though the battery start has given way to the rope pull start. (A smart, but unlucky, mouse decided that the fly wheel housing was a grand place to raise a family. Her children were still pre-schoolers when I started the engine to move the tiller out of the shed one day. Pieces of straw and feathers and other unmentionable bits suddenly flew out and explained why the motor stopped . . . and why

Ken now resorts to a rope pull.)

Organic Gardening magazine also said that clay was rich, needing only mulch. So mulch we did. We mulched with grass, with straw, with rotted alfalfa, with aquatic weeds raked out of the swimming area of the lake, with leaves and with garbage that we composted, or didn't compost as the notion struck us, and with manure, manure, manure. Ken shoveled truck loads, Kenny Tobias shoveled truck loads, Marty spread wagon loads with his spreader. It took years but we can now dig a two-inch trench, sprinkle seeds, and cover them with crumbly soil instead of "store bought" peat. We can walk in the garden and out again without a two pound accumulation of clay on each boot. Fat earthworms happily tunnel there in great numbers. Weeds can be pulled out by the roots instead of being scraped off by a sharp hoe.

A plot of reasonably "friable" soil is ours; one that produces quite well enough for our needs.

We thought that what we grew, we alone would eat. Not so. Other appetites stood waiting in the wings, watching our labors, wanting only to do the harvesting. Everything from aphids to deer and all sizes and kinds of critters in between. They had to be discouraged.

O.G. preaches purity of product, no chemicals, no poisons. Do it Nature's way. Be *organic*. Since the only defenses against deer are huge fences or bullets, we early decided to share with them. Their destruction has been minimal. A few things have been trampled as they take an occasional short cut through the garden to jump the fence into the big cornfield. The reason they prefer field corn to sweet corn is, in part, the result of our first break-through into the world of "natural" protection.

Ken had been hovering over his first anticipated crop of corn like a mother hen sitting anxiously on a nest of eggs soon to hatch. Every day or two he would check to see how full the little ears felt, and he was beginning to count in hours the time until he could pick the first ripe ones. This was to be the reward for the hours of hard labor he had put in to get them to the present state of near perfection. Then, one day, a trip to the corn patch revealed that Something Else was checking on the state of ripeness of the vegetable. The corn stalks at the edge of the garden were bent over and the ears were bitten into but not eaten. Tracks identified the culprit. Raccoons!

Organic Gardening to the rescue! One diabolically clever lady had written to the magazine her method for discouraging marauding creatures with a love of corn. I promptly tried it.

Directions: "Take a spray bottle of water, lace it heavily with tabasco sauce, and spray the ears of corn on the stalks on the perimeter of the plot. Repeat after a rain."

It was magic. The next time a raccoon tore into the husk to see if it was harvest time he got a mouthful that probably sent him scurrying to the lake for *water*! He lost all interest in our tabasco-flavored corn on the cob. The same thing, apparently, happened to the deer.

The corn was ours once it got to the bearing stage. To protect just planted or just sprouted seed from crows and other birds we strung clanking, shining aluminum pie tins on cords tied to forked sticks and stretched them across the garden over the emerging shoots. For reinforcement we use the birds' mortal enemy, the Snake. Toy serpents, coiled artistically between rows, look real enough to give visitors a start.

Bigger threats are the rabbits, who like things such as peas and lettuce and chard, at any stage of growth; and ground hogs, who have a nasty habit of waddling through, taking several big bites out of each tomato, squash, cabbage, cucumber or pumpkin that strikes their fancy. I'd like to thank the source of the solution to these problems, but I can't remember where it originated. It's weird and looks weirder but it seems to work. You do have to know a dog barber.

When I call Ginny Sines to make an appointment for our little dog Bandit's early spring shearing, I request that she save his hair and the hair from all the dogs she clips the day previous. These doggy smelling tangles I scatter around the garden edges. No rabbit or ground hog has yet crossed this odor barrier. More for appearances than need we also stick a few metal cat faces with green glowing eyes in between rows, in case some rabbit with sinus problems misses the warning canine aroma.

Cutworms are foiled by Ken's heavy scattering of wood ashes around the stalk of each young plant, but the majority of the insect world is undeterred by our organic efforts. Egg plants look lovely one day; the next, we find the leaves turned into lace by tiny leaf-hoppers. Next you'll see what had been a big, healthy tomato plant stripped of its leaves by a fat green tomato worm, hidden and waiting to have his next meal on another plant when our backs are turned. I enjoyed the pretty little dancing squadrons of white wings around the garden until I discovered they are called cabbage butterflies. As caterpillars, they are the crawling, voracious appetites that eat holes in the broccoli, cabbage and brussles sprout plants.

The prolific zucchini plant can be taking over the garden with its leafy vines one day and the next it has shriveled into a sad wilted thing. It has been attacked by a squash borer. This kind of sudden, senseless damage can give organic gardening a severe set-back. The dusts and sprays devised by modern science to cope with insect depradations seem quite reasonable.

By and large, though, we play by O.G.'s rules, with natural mulches and fertilizers. We enjoy the tasty results; not only from the garden, but from the red raspberry patch, the result of generous sharing by Celia and Charlie. An asparagus bed took seven years to produce and now gives us tender young shoots every spring. Nearby a rhubarb bed makes its annual offering.

All in all it is a joy, but the total result is, at times, overwhelming. 'Round about September the sealed jars have about filled the fruit cellar shelves and the deep freezes no longer yawn empty. I'm tired and hot and look from the kitchen door to see Ken coming up the hill from the garden. He is carrying a large bucket in each hand filled with the day's offering of ripe things to process: tomatoes, peppers, zucchini, Swiss chard, broccoli, peas and a few red raspberries in a cottage cheese container. It's a little much just then. But the year 'round pleasure that good "home grown" food gives us, and friends and relatives, does make the effort ultimately rewarding.

We no longer subscribe to *Organic Gardening* magazine. Ken says he can't handle any more suggestions for improvement in productivity. Neither can I.

Once the vegetable patch was established, Ken persuaded me to put in a flower bed in spite of my original declaration that I hadn't time to care for such things. In it, carefully tended, is Ken's Christmas present from some years ago, two plants billed as "Love Hollies," a male and a female for proper germination. The shiny leaves and red berries look nice in winter.

Not only are there more daffodils from my sister, but also her gifts of bright orange poppies, waxy yellow daisies and a clump of bergamont, or bee balm, that helps keep honey flowing for us.

A lovely columbine is the "thank you" from a dear and thoughtful niece for an hour of baby sitting.

Hummingbirds are constant visitors to the coral bells that wave delicately in the breezes most of the summer. They grow and flourish; and it pleases us to have them as a remembrance of the dear friend, now gone, who gave them to us.

Each year the forsythia grows long slender branches portending a huge clump of yellow sunshine to feast the eyes upon in the early spring. But, each winter the rabbits eat them in spite of every deterrent so far devised. About six yellow blossoms appeared one year on a tiny branch that the bunnies had missed, so hope continues.

The honeysuckle that produced such a sweet scent by the porch at the farm in Pennsylvania refuses to do more than grow as a tangle on the ground here where I transplanted a start of it. I keep insistently tying it to its support and hoping. It shades the grave of Robin 5, the poodle who was with me when we discovered the lake.

Mint, planted as an herb, has turned into a prolific weed that refuses to either stay in its spot or be eradicated. We've given up trying to control it and now enjoy mint jelly, mint tea, and, very happily, mint juleps.

Jerusalem artichoke and comfrey were more of my sister's

shared experimental plantings.

(She and *Organic Gardening* have had a happy life together. She plants in the friable soil of my childhood and could write little success stories for the magazine herself. My efforts in our stubborn clay are quite another matter.)

It is perplexing, however, that mint and comfry, for which we have little use, grow and flourish even in our soil. Jerusalem artichokes, too, started to grow and reproduce and edge out of their alloted spot. Then we discovered they were good raw in salads, as soup, and were, all in all, a superior vegetable. Since becoming useful, they don't seem nearly as prolific as they formerly were.

Grape arbors have romantic connotations. Gothic novels frequently mention them as trysting places for lovers. I thought a granddaughter growing up should have one as a place for pretending. Our friend and neighbor, George, agreed to help with its construction. The result is now a green-canopied little "room" made of eight foot cedar posts buried one and a half feet deep. Around and between them I made "walls" of chicken wire where growing grape tendrils cling. Extending from one side, a fence of more posts and wire take care of the grape vine overflow. The romantic look is achieved. In addition we have grape jelly, grape jam and grape juice all winter. A sister-in-law gets donations for her wine making efforts and some of it comes back by the bottle.

Where we live there are only five months of growing time. We try to make the days count.

Mother Nature, for all of her power and capriciousness, is a good provider, and some of the most satisfying "growing things" are those she cares for and nurtures herself. No need for us to dig or weed or fertilize. Just gather and enjoy.

First, in spring, are the elusive morel mushrooms. Elusive for us, that is. Local folks can, on occasion, walk our acres and find "a mess" for themselves and enough for us. This is frustrating in the extreme after we have walked, snail-paced, through these same areas for hours. These likely spots have been described to us by a dozen successful hunters. Unfortunately, each hunter seemed to be successful in a different place. Recommended morel habitats are: 1. Under old elms, 2. In old fruit orchards, 3. On the north slopes, 4. Under May apples, 5. Along fence rows, 6. In pine groves, 7. Under oak trees, 8. In deep woods. Our con-conclusion is that they might be found anywhere; so that's where we look, everywhere.

The results tend to be one or two mushrooms, stiff necks and frustrations. (Our frustration increased when good friends called saying they had found four morels in their front yard. They live in a Detroit suburb.) But we keep trying.

Perhaps part of the incentive is the recollection of a maga-zine article which stated that the going price for a pound of morel mushrooms was over $70. Since, until recently, no one has ever been able to discover how to domesticate them, the only source of these grotesquely ridged, up-side-down, cone-shaped tasties has been sharp-eyed, fanatic hunters, of whom there are thou-sands. Dick Kelchner, an old friend from Ohio, really got us started as morel fanciers. He used to have a helicopter and pilot at his disposal, theoretically for business purposes.

When spring arrived he always found reasons to fly to likely morel areas, starting south of his home state and each weekend moving a little farther north, well into Michigan. Until Dick took us hunting in our own latitude some years ago, neither of us had ever seen a morel.

At his suggestion we drove out in the country, down a back road, and suddenly Dick yelled, "Stop!" We piled out of the car, he pointed out what we were to pick and we came home with a half-bushel basketful, fried them in butter and were hooked. There had seemed to be nothing to it. Dick, like all experienced mushroom hounds, made it look easy. It isn't. You just keep try-ing until you get the hang of it.

Came the year that we found twenty in a gully not a hundred yards from our back door. Those twenty were the lesson that we needed. Mushrooms aren't quite so hard to see anymore. Better still, the frustration is gone. When we don't find them, we're now reasonably sure that there aren't any. Most springs we usually have at least one meal that includes morels.

There are dozens of kinds of mushrooms here; and while the morels are the most recognizable and exotic, there are a few others we do pick with confidence and eat with pleasure. Only a few that we know well and we don't fool with the others. *NO ONE SHOULD EVER EXPERIMENT WITH MUSHROOMS.*

The ones we're sure of include the odd-looking shaggy-mane, brown and white and delicious when they first emerge. But, as they age they ooze a black ink and dissolve.

The puffball was fun to find in the fields when we were little. If they were old and dry they would "puff" great smoky clouds of dark brown spores into the air when stomped on. We were still living in the city when we learned from a fellow urbanite that, when fresh, they are good to eat. The solid white meat, sliced in rounds, dipped in egg, dredged in flour and lightly sauteed in butter, is a real treat. Puffballs come in various sizes, from 2 to 14 inches and larger in diameter, and grow in rich deep humus.

Our favorite for all purposes is the meadow mushroom or "pink bottom" (because it grows in meadows and has a pink underside!). Our lawn, or more correctly, that large area around the house that we keep mowed, has been a wonderful source of these first cousins of the packaged mushrooms found in the grocery store's produce department. They mysteriously appeared one year, after a warm spring rain, and have reappeared several times both spring and fall ever since. It all started after Charlie's herd of cattle found a hole in the fence and came calling. Perhaps they brought the spores along on their visit. Whatever the reason, we are more than pleased, and enjoy these delicacies fried, in scrambled eggs, in soups, and on steaks. We've even strung them on strings and dried them when a long warm spell jumped production excessively.

KEN:

The last word on mushrooms is Shiitake. We read about them in *American Forestry* magazine. We inquired for more information at the local Extension office. We got the names of suppliers of Shiitake spores. This exotic species has been a part of oriental cuisine for centuries and now American enterprise is introducing it as a cash crop for marginal farmers, which is certainly what we are. Spurred on by reports of small fortunes to be made, we ordered a bit of the spore. Through some sort of misunderstanding, we ended up with three football-sized bags full of the stuff.

The next step was to enlist Marty in our bid for easy money. He agreed to cut the logs into which the spore must be introduced. Specifications are two to six inches in diameter, about four feet long and oak is preferred, although elm, ash and popple are also part of our experimental effort. Marty cut about twenty such logs (which must come from live trees), and, one spring morning, hauled them to our house. We set up a production line. He drilled as many 5/8-inch holes in each log as he could. Alice packed a bit of spore into each hole. I punched out seals of styrofoam from egg cartons and plastic cups, and they were plugged into the depressions to prevent errant floating spore from other mushrooms from mixing with our little thoroughbreds. After three hours of this, we had finished nine logs and about half of one of the three packages of spore. Marty hauled the rest of the logs home. Alice put the remainder of the spore in the refrigerator where it is supposed to last for five months.

To our amazement and delight we grew a delicious crop of Shiitakes right in that refrigerated bag! We were further pleased the following fall when these amazing goodies burst forth from the logs we had stacked in a nearby gully. Theoretically a crop can be gleaned every year for six consecutive years and fresh Shiitake mushrooms sell for as much as $6.00 a pound. A hundred pounds of logs, which is about what we impregnated, produce from 9 to 35 pounds a year. (Ours didn't, but we did get enough for some fine eating.)

Calculations indicate that if we would do a thousand logs we could make $9,250 in the second year of operation, and over a six-year period, excluding the cost of our labor, we could average more than $3,600 annually.

It's doubtful that we'll actually embark on such an enterprise, but it's nice to know what's possible.

ALICE:

One delicacy costs us no effort as spring days grow warmer. It's the eagerly awaited tantalizer, watercress. Just below the barn is an ever-flowing spring. It becomes a small stream that widens out on the flats edging the northwestern tip of the lake. It hustles around the willow tree roots, gurgles past a tangle of blackberry bushes, then slips by a walnut tree and into the rushes at the lake's edge. Containing just the right lime content, the water from that stream washes and nourishes the watercress. The little plants grow up and reach out in a thick blanket that almost conceals the stream in places. Tender, crisp and pungent, the cress is wonderful for salads, as a garnish, for soup. Sometimes we have it with with cream cheese on crustless bits of bread. We discovered that use when high tea was served at Dromoland Castle near Ireland's Shannon Airport!

Getting the cress to the kitchen can be challenging. Pictures sometimes show it being gathered by ladies in white dresses from the edges of burbling, firm-banked streams. That is not how we do it here. We wear old jeans and high boots and, with great caution, walk across the soggy flats and into ankle deep water. There is always the possibility of stepping into a particularly soft spot, in which case it is advisable to grab an overhanging limb and pull oneself out quickly. (One year one of Charlie's cows got all four feet stuck in the muck and, eventually, drowned. That knowledge acts as a great incentive for quick action.)

Once firm footing is found, we break off handsful of the tender green, taking three times the quantity we want.

Back at the house comes the tedious job of carefully inspecting each plant, discarding everything but the youngest, most tender stalks, and washing it thoroughly. Then it's soaked in strong salt water to eliminate tiny snails that the plant sometimes hosts. Then, crisp and cold, it's ready to enjoy.

I vividly recall one cress-gathering expedition.

Our friends, the Birnbryers, from Detroit had come for a weekend visit. Eddie went fishing with Ken, and I suggested to Dorothy that we take a walk through the little woods near the house. She could wait in the walnut grove while I gathered some watercress for lunch. The suggestion was accepted with great enthusiasm with one alteration. She wanted to pick watercress, too.

I explained the difficulties; but Dorothy was so interested that I found some boots of Ken's that would slip over her sneakers and hoped she would change her mind when she saw the locale. Not Dorothy. She clutched her plastic gathering bag and followed right behind me, carefully stepping right where I stepped. But, Ken's big boots made the already uncertain footing even more uncertain. She stumbled. She started to fall. She grabbed a sapling, a very young sapling. And it just gently bent over, lowering Dorothy down into the rich black muck of the flats. It *was* funny, and when I could control my mild hysterics, I helped her struggle to her feet. She was a sorry sight. Instead of wearing a pretty white dress for her cress picking, she had worn white shorts.

Months later she confided that she had tried every bleach her grocery store offered but none ever restored her shorts to their pristine beauty. She also mused that there must be *some* commercial value in a mud with such incredible and lasting color properties.

Next on Mother Nature's out-of-doors Give Away list are the wild strawberries of June. They are spoken about in every "back to nature" cookbook and magazine ever written. Their flavor is delicious, their smell divine. They are unique. That elusive taste has never been duplicated in any commercial berry. But they are so *tiny* and so fragile.

Nevertheless, every summer a strawberry picking expedition is launched with children and grandchildren equipped with small containers. There is continued optimism that they will bring back enough for cereal, for short cake, for ice cream, and maybe even jelly! Rarely have the contents of the containers, poured together, measured half-a-cup. Eating them while picking, and as refreshment on the walk back around the lake, is too temptingly pleasurable, evidenced by pink stained fingers and mouths, all around. No one ever wants to go back for more the next day. Next year is soon enough.

Dewberries are challenging. They, too, grow a few inches off the ground. They, too, are small, but in addition, they grow in a tight tangle of ankle-grabbing, briar-covered vines. Sometimes we just skip them.

Blackberries are much more satisfying in every way. Almost any neglected spot at a fence corner, a hedge row, at the edge of woods or swamps will eventually host some blackberries.

While they have vicious thorns, the canes grow tall which allows careful maneuvering and easy picking. They are bounteous beyond belief in those years when there has been a warm spring and a summer with plenty of rain. They can produce enough to take care of jelly, jam, frozen and canned needs for the next year or two when dry weather or a late spring freeze might destroy the fruit. In years of plenty we often "juice" them and freeze the result. On cold winter days it is a pleasure to warm the kitchen making jelly.

Even these abundant bushes can give happy surprises. One summer we wanted watercress just at the height of blackberry season. For the first time we looked at the tangle of blackberry canes growing at the edge of the stream and were astounded. The blackberries there were at least two or three times the size of ordinary wild berries. Picking them with delight, we froze them and for the next six months we would pull them out for display purposes before finally eating them. Many years before, Charlie's parents had a cabin at the top of the hill and down near the spring they had a garden. We suspect the giant berries were decendants of a few "store bought" plants they had nurtured.

A half gallon plastic milk jug is traditional berry picking equipment around here. With the top cut out so as to leave the handle firmly intact, it can be tied to the waist with a belt. This leaves both hands free to pick the fruit.

Once, when Ken and I were both picking, I had just about filled my jug when a shouted "Hello!" announced Ken's approach. Answering him to guide him to my spot, I chortled to myself. Wouldn't *he* be surprised to see all my berries.

The surprise was mine. He had *two* jugs, both full. Going clear to the south east corner of the property, he had found a lovely big growth of canes bearing more of those *huge* berries. These had to have been planted by bird droppings. No dooryard or garden on record was ever near that spot.

We've found a few wild black raspberries growing in the fence row around the house. They are wonderful when they, like the blackberries, have had the kind of season that produces fat fruit.

Ken became enamored of elderberries early in our marriage.

It was when my mother brought a dusty bottle of elderberry wine out of the cellar of the farm house. Ken pronounced it splendid, as he did the bottle of dandelion wine she brought up next. I don't remember what it tasted like. I was too shocked to remember. During all my growing-up years while mother gave warnings, and told horror stories of people she knew who *drank*, those bottles of *alcohol* were sitting in some dark corner of our house aging away! She defensively explained she'd made the wine for medicinal purposes. I later learned that elderberry juice was a favorite remedy of the ancient Greek doctor, Hippocrates, though I haven't discovered if he allowed it to ferment first.

My own later attempts to make either kind of wine were total failures (unless Ken is right when he says our dandelion wine was an excellent paint remover!)

The elderberries we now pick each season make lovely pies and jellies and elderberry pancakes. In late fall we drive along our back roads looking for the tall bushes growing at the edges of swampy areas. It is a quick job to fill our gathering bags with the plate-shaped umbrels of black fruit.

The time consuming task is stemming the tiny berries for

freezing in plastic bags, which Ken is *much* better at than I.

Last on the list of wild fruits that we enjoy are wild blueberries, or huckleberries. As far as we're concerned it takes a botanist to know the difference. Whatever called, they are so good to the taste and so pleasant to pick. An hour or two in the cool moist shade of the swamps, where they grow in profusion, is a treat if you've remembered to take along mosquito repellent. Wild blueberries have a firmer texture and a flavor quite different than that of the cultivated species. There are several "Pick-UR-Own" commercial blueberry patches in the area. The berries are about twice as big as the wild ones and by late fall it's fun to fill the remaining empty spots in the freezers with *easily* picked fruit.

It is only after the first two or three frosts in the fall that you should gather the last of nature's bounty, the nuts. The most fun is the black walnut. They are so big that it takes no time to fill a bushel basket full. Next comes the task of removing the thick, soft outer husk. A friend offered the use of her corn sheller saying it stripped the husks off very satisfactorily. Others recommend a driveway and car traffic to do the job. Sometimes that does a total destruct. So I've devised my own, rather outlandish method.

Donning rubber boots, I do a "walnut dance" on the spread-out pile of nuts. A pressured slide and twist loosens the thick covering, then with my hands encased in bread wrappers, I do the final undressing. (Walnut stained furniture is socially acceptable. Walnut stained hands are not.)

If Ken hasn't turned off the outside faucet for the winter by the time this operation is complete, the nuts get a hosing. In any event, they must dry for a month or so before the hard work begins, the work my father used to do.

When winter had put his fields to sleep, he would sit sit in our cellar, an iron shoe last between his knees, and crack nuts for my mother's baking. He never let me swing the big hammer, though it *looked* easy, as it always does when you're a child. The first time I tried cracking ours, I quickly found out that just being "grown-up" doesn't make black walnut cracking any easier.

When I complained to Ed McPharlin about the difficulty of finishing the walnut harvest, he made no comment. Later he called with an address and a suggestion that we should order the proper tool if we wanted to cut down on the work of cracking nuts. We did, though the price seemed a mite extreme. We could have gotten four hammers for the price of the cracker, but, Ed's suggestions were always good ones.

This was no exception. A few weeks after we sent our order a very heavy package arrived. It contained a large metal ratchet, designed with a welded handle. This device makes cracking any nut, large or small as easy as shelling a peanut. Ours delighted us so much, that we got one for my dad. When age kept him out of his fields and barn, he could still enjoy cracking the black walnuts that fell from the old tree just off the corner of his back porch.

There are other nuts on our place. Hickories are favorites with our squirrel neighbors. Even if the nuts are small and don't have the highly flavored meat of the black walnut, it's nice to have enough of them to make a hickory nut cake.

Then, there's the big butternut tree that we discovered one fall. The nuts are mild and rich with the buttery flavor their name implies and much too good to be left entirely to our tree-dwelling neighbors. The meats are fragile and more difficult to extract than any of the others, but worth the effort.

Out of curiosity we've tried other wild edibles. Dandelion greens and poke, in season, are great. Dandelion flowers, fried, are terrible. Cattail roots, boiled, are tolerable.

The berries and nuts, the mushrooms and watercress, those are staples that came with the farm, free and bountiful gifts from the invisible proprietor who really runs the place. In this age of warnings about insidious chemicals, suspicious sprays and powders and their effect on store-bought foods, it's nice to have an ample supply of Mother Nature's Own.

14

Bridging the Generation Gap

KEN:

ONE OF THE WONDERS of life in the country is the way it homogenizes generations. Fishing enthusiasts, farmers, hunters, flower lovers, hikers, gardeners, come in all ages, and when they are doing their things no one seems to notice or care about birthdays. Granted, younger legs get over the fences faster, but older heads often know the best places to go for everything from deer stands to berry patches. Non-contemporaries don't compete, they complement each other. It all goes back to the family farm tradition, the apportionment of work that takes into consideration the abilities and capacities of all concerned. Patriarchs and matriarchs are still very much part of the rural pattern and the wisdom of years seems more respected on the backroads than in the marts of trade.

Just having this place has given us the chance, even the need, to stay related to our juniors. Once they came as children of our friends, brought along, willy-nilly, "to visit the Joneses." Then, as their interests parallel ours, they come because they want to share what's here.

It is that way with Todd Kelchner. His parents, Dick and Mary Ellen, had been part of our courtship days at Clarion College. We had been in their wedding party, they had visited us at our first home. Now Dick is a very successful contractor and road builder in Dayton, Ohio. Therefore, when we were planning this place it seemed only sensible to get his advice on the construction of the long driveway into our house site, and, naturally, he and his family had to come and check it out. It was a short visit, but it did the trick. The next summer came a call. It was Mary Ellen.

"Hi, just checking in. How are things?"

"Great," Alice told her, "Say, it's your turn to visit. Want to come to the lake?"

"Well, no, not right now, I've got a golf tournament and Dick has just started a big job for the city of Dayton. But Todd would *love* to come. Could he?"

Todd was thirteen. Alice was startled, but game.

"I suppose so. Won't he get bored with just Ken and I?"

Mary Ellen was prepared.

"We thought of that. He'd like to bring Johnny."

That was Todd's best friend. He had visited the lake before.

Ken picked the boys up at the nearest airport on a Thursday afternoon. Before sundown they were unpacked, briefed on boundaries and safety precautions, and *gone*. Subsequently the only time we would see them close up was at meals. Otherwise they were out on the lake in the old rowboat, walking the shoreline with long-handled fishnets over their shoulders, wandering the meadows and woods. They delivered fresh caught bluegills for a fish fry. They came in late and exhausted, to sleep, and were out and gone before the next morning's breakfast. We delighted, vicariously, in the pleasures of youth.

During the following years we lost track of Johnny, who had a troubled adolescence. Once his parents called. The boy had run away and they thought he might have come to the lake.

It was, they said, his favorite place in the world.

Todd came back a few times, with his folks, but hockey, college, and a growing part in his father's business kept him busy. We traveled half way across the country to attend the wedding of Todd and Lisa and had a wonderful time. Years flew by, as they do.

Then one day came another phone call. This time it was Dick.

"You a grandpa yet?" I asked, rudely.

"No, but hoping," Dick said. Then he told me that he and Todd had been working very hard, that Lisa's medical practice had worn her down and that the three of them were looking for a restful weekend.

"He's always wanted to show her your place," Dick concluded, "and this seems like a good time."

That it did and they arrived late Friday. We installed the couple in the guest house where they could be to themselves while we reminisced. Again, we saw little of our young guests. They were out in the boat, fishing, walking the shoreline with nets, wandering the woods and meadows. The weather was fine, Alice outdid herself in terms of cuisine, and the whole time was relaxing, pleasant, refreshing.

It was just about nine months hence when Dick and Mary Ellen became grandparents. We're hoping that, in the not too distant future the phone will ring.

"Todd, calling," the familiar voice will say. "Jeff's big enough to go fishing. Lisa and I would like to show him your place."

Business is a breeding ground for casual acquaintanceships, but gives birth to few real friendships. One of the most prized continuations of our former life is our relationship with Bill and June Walker. Bill is a brilliant composer and pianist. We worked together on dozens of jingles, musical backgrounds and themes for many advertisers. Together, we wrote and composed a musical that almost made it to Broadway. June, an Australian, was Bill's war bride from Brisbane, and is a truly remarkable woman.

They live in the famous Winslow House, Frank Lloyd Wright's first commissioned home in River Forest, Illinois.

June has lavished work and love and care on the place and it should be a national monument. Once the four of us went around the world together and collected memories for a lifetime. The Walkers have three boys. The youngest is Peter. The first time his father visited the lake, on business, Peter came along.

While Bill and I discussed lyrics and melodies, Alice looked after Peter. There was certainly no problem with boredom. He was interested in everything that crept, crawled, hopped or wriggled. By evening he had filled all available empty milk cartons and cottage cheese containers with lizards, salamanders, worms, pollywogs, frogs, crayfish, and small snakes. He insisted on taking them home, to his father's considerable discomfiture.

Even though they were packed in the trunk, they might escape and find their way to the front seat. That didn't worry Peter. He climbed in back, stretched out, and dreamed of his treasures all the way back to River Forest.

Bill and June love their home, understandably. He has converted an old coach house into a studio, the country club is nearby, theirs is the ideal suburban life. But, on occasion, we have coaxed them into a weekend in the country. Peter always came along enthusiastically. Once, a late start got them to Aurohn Lake well after midnight. Beds were ready and a good night's sleep would assure a Saturday full of country pleasures. That was not to be.

As soon as the car door opened Peter was out, shouting:

"*Look at those stars!* Did you ever see anything like it?"

We do have nice stars and, because there are no city lights to diminish them, they seem bigger and brighter to urbanites.

Peter had come prepared to take full advantage of his unusual opportunity. From the back of the station wagon, he emerged with some large pieces of equipment. While we were moving luggage inside he set up a large telescope outside.

"Instead of bugs," June explained, "he's now interested in astronomy."

Only when cloud cover arrived just before dawn, did Peter go to bed. All elements fascinate Peter Walker. When he was sixteen, shortly after he obtained his driver's license, he and a friend made the trip to the lake. Barely taking time for introductions all around, the two boys began hauling gear from the rear of the station wagon. This time water was the environment to be explored. They had wet suits, gloves, boots, fins, face masks, aqua lungs and tanks of oxygen. They were ready to plumb the depths. Our lake's twenty feet was hardly a challenge, so, with permission from Charlie, they plunged into neighboring Whitefish Lake. Hearsay has it that a plumb line was dropped a hundred feet deep into these natural, glacial waters and it never touch bottom!

When our intrepid divers reached forty feet, they'd had enough. The cold springs that feed Whitefish numbed their bones and their enthusiasm. But what a day they had, and what an adventure for us, too.

Peter, with boundless energy, enthusiasm and ambition completed Amherst, became a skilled musician, did well in business. He married Vicki, a marvelous girl whose capabilities match his. At first they lived in a very noisy condominium in downtown Chicago. They came to see us one weekend. Peter, as always, leaped from his car. As soon as Vicki had exited, too we welcomed them.

Peter had his intense look.

"Listen!" he cried.

We did. We didn't hear anything extraordinary. The three of us looked inquiringly at Peter.

"Listen to the silence!"

We hope starlight and silence will bring Peter and Vicki back. Maybe, someday, here, they can introduce their children to the creatures and constellations of the country.

So many old friends and colleagues have come and brought us memorable moments.

Don and Barbara Tennant shared our early days in Chicago advertising. Don is an action guy. If things need doing, he likes to see them done. A few years ago the Tennants came for a couple of days, and we showed them our new island. It's tiny and round, with a moat around it, and it's called Alice Island. We claim it's where all immigrants must land and register before coming ashore. As a sort of artifact, on the island, we had rigged the old, original, red rowboat that Ken Granata had given us. It leaked badly, by now, and the wooden gunwales were rotting, but, like the wrecks of old schooners, it had an air of romance about it. It was, however, rather in the way when we swam and fished. So I said to Don:

"We've got to get rid of that old boat."

Don was in the Navy during World War II and he looked at the wreck like it was a Japanese carrier.

"Let's sink it," he said. "Let's take it out to the middle of the lake and sink it."

It sounded easy, and there were two of us, so, why not?

We wrestled it off the beach and into the water, and trickles seeped in around the seam between the wooden sides and the metal floor.

"We'd better hurry," I cautioned. "If it gets too full, we'll never get it out to the middle."

"You'd better bring along an axe," Don suggested. "In case we need it."

Using a new rowboat and a tow rope, we pulled the sluggish wreck out to the middle.

It wouldn't sink. It sat, slightly submerged, but wouldn't sink.

Don got irritated. He clambered out of our boat and boarded Old Red, axe in hand. He hacked at the thin sheeting of the floor, punched more holes in it.

"Listen, Don, you'd better get out of there. It's going to sink," I warned him.

"Damn right it is," he muttered, and clambered back into the good craft.

Old Red settled slowly at the stern, but the bow stayed up like a whale's snout, pointing skyward. Don leaned perilously far from our boat. He pushed. He poured a steady stream of invective over the old red nose as it settled into the lake. Now some air bubbles boiled to the surface. With a kind of gulp, Old Red disappeared. Out there, somewhere, it's a hiding place for bass and bluegills.

I hummed "Anchors Aweigh" as we rowed back to Alice Island. Don looked downright victorious. Maybe, one day, he and Barbara will bring child, or grandchild to this scene of triumph. We hope so.

Dear old neighbors come to see us, too.

Shortly after we were married, we bought a house, a log house, thirty miles southwest of St. Louis. Our post office was House Springs, and in that tiny town there was a newly opened "mom and pop" grocery store.

It was owned and operated by our neighbors on Duda Road, Vic and Della Nahlik. With them and their five-year old son, "Chum," we had barbecues and picnics, card games and dancing and all the fun of being young. In time we moved away but, ever so often, we'd visit our old home and all the people there. The little store became a supermarket. "Chum" grew into West Pointer, Charles, and had a younger brother, Steve.

By the time we bought the lake, Charles was off to war in Vietnam, and we thought a visit and a vacation might divert his worried parents. We invited them and, with Steve, they came *loaded for fish*. The Nahliks are fishing nuts. They love the sport and pursue it vigorously. They showed up with half-a-dozen rods, three tackleboxes, and a huge assortment of Missouri worms dug up around store and home. They even brought catfish bait, some sort of noxious stuff guaranteed to catch the whiskered bottom feeders.

From the afternoon that they arrived until the day of departure, we caught fish. Bass, bluegills, sunfish, catfish, we pulled them into the boat, up on the dock and the dam, all along the shoreline. We ate fresh fish, froze pounds of them to be transported back to Missouri.

An annual event had started.

Charles came back from Vietnam, thin, tired, nervous. He came to see us at the farm and fished. He also trimmed willows, cut grass, repaired the dock. He loved being here and we loved having him. We talked about his wife, Carol, about their three daughters, Mary, and the twins, Susie and Sandy.

The next summer, when Vic called, he asked:

"Say, do you mind if Charles comes along and brings the twins? They could stay in the guest house and wouldn't be any bother."

Agreed.

Charles and his teen-agers took over the guest house, and he rigged a communications system between the two buildings. The girls fished, but, like their father, they were workers. Their idea of fun was operating our riding lawn mower or helping their dad prune trees and burn brush. Such guests we should always have!

Every year they've been back until summer jobs for college tuition interfered. Both the girls, however, have mentioned that this would be a nice place for a honeymoon.

Who knows? Unto the fourth generation, maybe?

Another "regular" is Rick, just finishing his senior year in college, six feet plus and 190 pounds, a fine student and ex-football player. He's the youngest son of Linda, Alice's niece. She, her husband, Rodger Ackinclose, and their two boys, Randy and Rick, came every summer for a while, lived in the guest house, and made good use of the lake. Then business and other activities broke the schedule and they couldn't make it. Except for Rick. One summer he boarded a bus in Pittsburgh, rode all night. I met him at the bus station, suitcase and all. He set up his bachelor quarters in the guest house, spread out clothes, fishing gear, potato chips, fritos, pop, transistor radio, and all. He and Alice talked a lot about the family in Pennsylvania. He and I fished and didn't say too much. But, somehow, we were communicating. Now Rick drives the four hundred and fifty miles to the lake each summer and we have our week together.

Nephew Mike brings his son, Benjamin, to fish. Grand-nephew Scott bags his first deer. Niece Claire comes all the way from Washington State. It's all part of staying in touch with tomorrow.

Happily there are new and younger friends who also share the place.

Jay and Karen come at least once a year and help us plant trees on Mitcheney Point. (Her name was Mitchell, his, Sweeney and they combined them to name a little peninsula.)

Jack and Susie, country dwellers, too, and fellow members of the Charlie Tobias fan club come often. Marty and Sue Preston and their three kids, Ann Marie, Kristi and Scott, are part of our lives.

They all make us feel so young.

Then there's the growing college crowd. The graduate students who have been my teaching assistants have all come and come again. Jan Wicks, her husband, Rob; Tom Ennis, Neal Yonover, Steve Coppola, Joni Park, Ajili Hodari, Zach Mathew, all have been over and they find it a welcome break from campus business, even though it's a fifty-mile drive. They've fished and hiked, stayed late and talked. Alice has to warn me to ease up on the invitations, so we'll have some time to ourselves.

We have an increasing list of animal friends, too. Dogs and cats tag along with weekend visitors. The Dudleys brought a comical dog named Goober and a cat called C.D. The initials stood for Character Deficiency. It was a strange cat.

Joe and Sandy Loving are the very proud possesors of not one, but *two* Black Labradors who have been our house guests. Blue and Murphy walk about gently in the house and intimidate our small dog, Bandit, who sits in a chair where he can look them in the eye. Once outside, the Labs are in Heaven, dashing into the lake and doing the kind of swimming for which they are bred.

Jay and Karen announced, once, that they were bringing their new puppy to visit. Pepper proved to be a sixty pound airedale with huge paws. He had an endearing way of resting his chin on the dining room table and his paw on Bandit's back. The table held up, but Bandit collapsed.

One young couple, friends of our son's, came in a van with a brace of Siberian Huskies. They weren't allowed to roam and protested their incarceration with wolflike howls during much of a very long night.

Drasko and Marge Vidic were attended by a well-trained and intensely loyal German Shepherd. It was so loyal, in fact, that it followed the row boat when D. and I went fishing. His proximity made casting difficult and we decided he should be in the boat. Pulling a large animal into a small craft is a risky exercise in seamanship. We were as wet as the dog by the time he was aboard. Years later, it all happened over again, with Tom Ennis and his ancient golden retriever, Taffy. She, too, would follow him anywhere and we had to haul all sixty pounds of her over the side and into the boat.

It was always something of a breather when the Ashtons came, with pet. First it was Topsy, a miniature poodle, then Dolly, a Lhasa Apso. Both liked to stay in the house.

It seems probable that should Blue, or Murphy, or Pepper, or any of our animal friends have progeny, they too, will run free for a while at Aurohn Lake.

What's sauce for the people is sauce for their pets.

It seems unlikely that we'll ever be lonesome as long as we're in residence here.

15

From Faraway Places

KEN:

DURING THE overseas assignment to which we have previously alluded, we tended to romanticize our place in the country. In fact, before we left, and with the long separation in mind, we constructed a photo mural that was terrific. It was a composite of three 35 millimeter slides taken from one spot high on a hill at the west end of the lake. Paul Wonsack, an art director buddy of mine, put them together and had the result enlarged to a picture about two and a half feet long and a foot high. It was really impressive and it hung on the walls of our temporary homes in Sydney and Singapore. When we had guests, they would invariably ask about the big portrait of a lake, and we would launch into tales of our adventures there and would invariably end up saying:

"If you're ever in the States, you must come see us."

Little did we know.

Located as we are in the middle of the country, far from Disneyland, Niagara Falls, the Great White Way, Yellowstone, Grand Canyon and other stellar attractions, we thought we were just being friendly when we uttered the invitation. Surely no one would go out of their way to visit a little farm near a small town in the rural upper Midwest.

Guess again.

One fascinating assignment during the stay in Southeast Asia was working for the Beecham's account in Kuala Lumpur, Malaysia. That meant figuring out how to advertise Brylcreem, Enos Salts, Horlicks and other English-originated products to a mixed market of Chinese, Malaysians, Indians, Eurasians and Europeans. The man in charge of the whole operation was John Robb, an astute Scotsman.

He discharged his responsibilities so well that some time later he was made vice-president of Beecham's North American operation with headquarters in New Jersey. By that time we were in full-time residence at Aurohn Lake. The phone rang one day.

"Kensinger," the voice said in beautiful, burred tones, "John Robb here."

I was surprised and delighted. John explained that another promotion had come his way and he was being posted back to London, the home office of Beecham's.

"Before we leave the U.S. in May," he concluded, "there are three things we intend to do. Visit Disneyland, see Niagara Falls and spend a few days at the Jones Estate."

I wondered, briefly, if I had overstated the splendors of our place.

"Delighted to have you," I said, "Just let me check the calendar with Alice."

After hurried consultation we suggested mid-April.

"Fine," John said, "There will be Janet and myself and the children. You remember them, Angus, Neal and Jane, don't you?"

"Of course," I agreed, although my recollection was limited to flashes of them on their way to bed, passing through large parties of celebrating people.

"We'll plan to arrive on the Monday after we see the Falls," John is a careful planner, "and leave on the Saturday following."

"Fine," I enthused, "We'll look forward to it."

"One other thing," John sounded a bit tentative, "Could you arrange for Gordon Rothrock to come up? He's challenged me to a game of golf, and I thought perhaps we could squeeze that in during our visit. Maybe on Friday."

Gordon was president of our International Company and was headquartered in Chicago, a hundred and eighty miles away.

"I'll see what I can do," I said.

Alice looked askance and simply said "Oh!" when I described the Robb's timetable. She then asked me if I recalled that I was leaving for a trout fishing weekend with my brother on the day before the Robbs planned on leaving. I hadn't, but I was sure it would all work out O.K.

T. S. Eliot had it right when he wrote, "April is the cruelest month of all." The day before our guests arrived, the weather, which had been balmy and promising, did an abrupt switch, dropped the temperature sharply and started delivering the showers that go with the month.

"Don't worry about it," I suggested to my wife, "This kind of weather is typical of Scotland. They'll feel right at home."

That turned out to be quite true. Within hours of their arrival we were Uncle Ken and Aunt Alice to Angus, Neal and Jane. John is a determined, yet flexible, guy and he wanted to take advantage of every hour of their time. It was misty, if not rainy, when we launched the two rowboats. John had, I believe, been an officer in the Royal Navy and he used nautical terms as he introduced the two little boys to the art of oar-pulling. Jane and I in the other boat watched the exercise with interest and a touch of apprehension. The little instructional craft had a tendency to rock violently when the two youngsters traded seats. When I expressed concern John used the phrase that I had heard so often in Australia.

"Not to worry," he said, "They can both swim."

After another adventurous and somewhat damp day Janet, John's wife, decided that, as long as she was in the midwest, she would like to see our Second City, Chicago.

"The Rothrocks are coming for golf, aren't they?" she asked.

I had, subsequent to John's request, arranged that. I had also called the local Golf Club, of which I am not a member (I abhor golf) and arranged for John and Gordon to have their game as scheduled. So I had to agree.

"Well," said Janet in her matter-of-fact way, "Couldn't I fly to Chicago, do some shopping, stay overnight with them, and then couldn't we all drive back here together?"

I could think of no reason to say it was impossible. There was, indeed, a morning flight from the nearby airport. A phone call confirmed space on it, and, in due course Janet vanished. For two days Alice was mother to us all. On the third day Janet resurrected, along with Gordon and Barbara, and that night, to continue a biblical analogy, there was very little room at the inn. Seven bodies, in addition to our own wearying bones, pretty well filled all available mattresses. It was still too cold for anyone to sleep comfortably in our non-winterized guest house. Using fold-a-beds, couches and cots, we somehow got everybody horizontal, if not entirely comfortable. After all guests were in bed, Alice and I looked at the beautiful burnished copper pitcher that Janet had brought us as a house gift found on her Chicago shopping tour.

"It's a nice thing to remember them by, isn't it?" I suggested.

"Yes," Alice agreed, then, cryptically, "Not that I'll really need it."

On Friday, as scheduled, I left to meet my brother for our annual opening day trout fishing trip. When I departed John and Gordon were somewhere around the fourth hole on the local golf links; Angus, Neal and Jane were fishing, and Alice, Janet and Barbara were having late coffee. Later, as the weather finally turned sunny, Alice took the ladies and the kids for a tour of the place in the Jeep truck. When the golfers returned John delivered a treasured pronouncement.

"That course," he said, "was delightful. Reminded me very much of St. Andrews."

High praise indeed to be favorably compared with Scotland's mecca for followers of the little white ball. It was a fine capstone to a splendid vacation at the Jones Estate, declared John.

"I love your place and I loved Chicago," Janet said.

"It was nice of you to have us over. How beautiful it is. You must love it here," the Rothrocks expressed their sentiments.

Of course this was all unheard by me. I was following a dry fly along a wilderness river when these sentiments were uttered just before check out time at Aurohn Lake on Saturday morning. Alice responded graciously and we promised to visit the Robbs the next time we were in England. We still hear from them nearly every Christmas and they reiterate the invitation. Some day we'll get there.

Their unforgettable sojourn was the first of many responses to the offhand invitations I had uttered overseas. Some were planned and expected. Others were complete surprises.

Like the one that started with this telephone conversation.

"Rob Taylor here," the voice said in unmistakably Australian accents.

"Hello, Rob," was the best I could do. The name rang no bells of recollection.

"I'm a friend of Ann Murray's," he said. The Murrays had been our neighbors in Northbridge, the Sydney suburb where we enjoyed life for more than a year. Ann was a very attractive daughter.

"Good on you," I quipped to indicate I spoke his language.

"They speak highly of you, the Murrays do," he flattered.

"They were great neighbors." I responded.

"Said you had a beaut place in the country," Rob pursued it.

"Nice of them. We showed them our pictures." I could see it coming so I got ahead of it. "Why don't you have a look yourself?"

That's the kind of instinctive sentence that has kept us gregarious. Rob showed up the next day in a five-year old white Falcon that had already criss-crossed the United States twice, once north, once south and now right down the middle, as he put it. Rob, in his late twenties, had resigned a very good job with a major brewer and set out to see the world with his savings.

Wanted to do it before he settled down, supposedly, at this juncture, with Ann. It was a beautiful midsummer's day when he arrived and he was utterly captivated. He efficiently stowed his gear in the guest house and disappeared for about ten minutes. When he emerged it was in very brief shorts, a T-shirt and tattered sneakers.

"I'll just have a look about," he said, "Anywhere I shouldn't go?"

I told him where the fence lines were and watched him saunter off towards the dam. What a joy it was to watch him and join him for the next few days. He stocked up on cereal and milk for the refrigerator in the guest house and would breakfast quietly and early. Before the sun was all the way up he would be out in the canoe, fishing, or simply observing. He was excited by the wild life, a deer, a muskrat, a chattering squirrel, all were events to Rob. How many times he said:

"I could never imagine a place like this."

It's true. In the water-poor land of Australia the idea of a self-contained, owned lake in the outback is, to coin a phrase, outlandish. What's more, when you gambol about the countryside there, you do so at considerable risk. There are the snakes, for instance. When I told Rob that ninety-nine percent of the reptiles he might see around our place were perfectly harmless, he was amazed.

"At home," he said, and we knew it to be true, "it's just the other way around."

"No funnelweb spiders, no bloody wood ticks, it's a paradise," Rob chortled as he made off to the woods, barelegged and sneaker shod. That's the way he went into the huckleberry swamp with Alice when she went picking one day. He loved the squish of mud between his toes knowing that there would be no leeches on his feet when they emerged.

We could sense his real regret when it was time to say goodbye. We watched the old white car crest the hill, caught his wave out the side window just before he disappeared. Three weeks later we had a postcard from him. He was on his way up the

Amazon River, intending to follow it to its source. His freedom fling lasted long enough for his understanding with Ann to end so we lost track of him. We would love to see him again and watch him use every hour of every waking day in the pursuit of the pleasures he found so excitingly available.

Another year, Ann's parents, our old Northbridge neighbors, Cameron and Sheila, decided to do an extended tour of the U.S. and Canada and we were on their itinerary for early fall.

"We'd love to see your famous autumn colors," Sheila wrote, "When they are at their glorious best."

They arrived on October 5th and it was raining. The trees were dank and colorless and the thermometer registered around fifty degrees Fahrenheit or eighteen Celsius, which is how Australians measure temperature. By any measurement it was miserable, and we fired up the wood stove to take off the chill and add a note of cheer. It was an inauspicious start for their ten-day sojourn. Plucky people, however, were our guests, undiscouraged by the elements.

We visited the barn during a drizzle, walked the woods with a damp fog for atmosphere, had a wine and cheese picnic as the temperature flirted with freezing. One day, on a drive, we found a small swamp where some accident of nature had turned the leaves on half-a-dozen trees to scarlet and yellow.

"They're beautiful," enthused Sheila, "I can imagine what it's like when all the forest looks that way."

"Lovely," Cameron nodded vigorously, "They must be lovely."

In the eyes of those delightful beholders Fall had officially arrived. They had seen the colors.

Our next guests from Down Under were far more fortunate. They caught the last days of a particularly beautiful summer. A warm September sun made fishing and float boating fun for Ralph and Janet Peverill from Alice Springs.

They had fled Melbourne twenty years before and moved to Australia's only interior town. He was a cartoonist and animator and could do his work in the remotest place, handle deliveries by mail, visit the cities only when business demanded it. We had met them in Singapore where he did some work for one of our advertising clients.

During dinner at Raffles Hotel we had uttered the casual invitation to "come see us if you're ever in the states." Sure enough, here they were. Ralph had developed a very funny cartoon strip called Outer Space and decided to take it, personally, to the syndicated services in New York. They had spent a miserable week in the Great Metropolis, having pre-arrranged conferences cancelled, being treated rudely by officious receptionists and learning that the great distance they had traveled was of little moment to the buyers of comics.

Ralph made it clear that, in a sense, they looked upon their visit with us as a place to nurse a few wounds to the ego and blows to the ambition. He donned a Malay sarong that was his usual loafing outfit back in Alice Springs and sought a quiet place to sit and contemplate the lake. While he invited his soul, Janet turned out to be a hiker without peer. She and Alice did the woods and the fields, the pastures, barn and marsh. They checked out the cows and startled a deer and stirred up innumerable chipmunks. They had a perfectly marvelous time. By the third day Ralph was recovering his creative urges and we, together, began to construct a menagerie in our minds.

It was filled with creatures like The Biteless Flird, The Petulant Paycock, The Wide-Eyed Zapzucker and other creatures who inhabited a place called the Zycho-Zoo. He did cartoons and I did doggerel and we thought we might have the makings of a book. His sketches were sharp and hilarious and better than my verses. He drew a group of little, birdlike creatures clustered in a nest under the watchful eye of a large female. A nestling was poised on the edge, about to leave. We called it the Tiny Tufted Tithanger and its proclivities were rhymed:

It hates to leave its habitat,
And seldom strays from home.
The family clings together

In a small, inverted dome.
At least two generations
Dwell within the nest,
An old female is the leader
Her cry is "Mom knows best."
When a young one tries departure
With a vig'rous, lusty bound
Mother bird collapses
With a sobbing, sighing sound.
It stops the young cock in his tracks
And turns him right around
So he stays a little longer,
She's happy, he's unmated.
It's a mystery how this species
Ever stays perpetuated!

These efforts cheered Ralph, if nothing else. By departure time he was refreshed in spirit. We continued the collaboration by letter for months and our projected book got fatter. We even got it copyrighted and tried it on a couple of publishers. Although they've never been printed the pictures are good for chuckles still.

Now Ralph and Janet have their own acreage just outside of Alice Springs, a place they call El Cerrito. We're invited and would love to go, preferably in August. That's when these dwellers in one of the world's most arid regions hold a boat race. Ralph sent me a first-day postal cover featuring the event. On the envelope it proclaims the Henley-on-Todd race, the "Original, world famous annual waterless regatta held on the dry bed of the Todd River, Alice Springs, in Central Australia." That should be worth seeing.

When Kristi Koh, our tiny, beautiful friend and former colleague from Singapore made her first trip to the U.S.A., we were on her itinerary. She flew into a major airport that is a good two hours away from our house.

Now her whole country is about twenty-six miles long and

can be completely traversed in an hour. So, as we droned along the freeway, heading home, she expected reasonably quick arrival. After the first seventy miles she said, piquantly:

"Ken Jones, where are you taking me?"

She repeated the question when we passed the hundred mile mark. I just smiled at her and said:

"You'll see."

Visions of kidnapping, she later admitted, flashed through her mind when we hit the winding gravel road near home. It's a fair distance between houses and on the island where Kristi lives nearly two million people occupy half the space of our whole county with its forty thousand souls. It was becoming a long, lonesome ride and she literally squealed with delight when we crested the hill and she saw the house and lake. Suddenly there was plenty of population.

Alice was hostess to the ladies of the local chapter of the American Association of University Women and their husbands. There were introductions and conversation all around. Kristi, for a while, became the focal point of the party. Then, suddenly, she vanished. A short time later the doorbell rang. We opened the front door and there she was, breathtaking in a long, embroidered Chinese gown, and carrying an exquisitely wrapped package. She bowed.

"Thank you for extending to me the hospitality of your home," she said.

This was her proper, planned and gracious Oriental entrance.

Alice unwrapped and shook out an intricate, hand dyed wall hanging from Indonesia and, good friends though they were, every club member there suffered a brief twinge of envy. The riches of the East had come to our rural living room.

Kristi enjoyed the riches of the midwest the next day as Aurohn Lake performed for her. A deer and a spotted fawn leaped out of a brush pile just ten feet in front of our little all-terrain vehicle as we toured the south pasture. Two Great Blue Herons who might have been at home in a Chinese tapestry flapped sedately upwards as we skirted the marsh. A float boat cruise was cut short by the appearance of thunderheads on the western horizon and an ominous, distant rumbling. We were just up the hill and in the door as big drops splattered the patio. Then we had a brief, furious monsoon-like storm that was, for all the world, like the summer downpours we had all experienced, together, in Singapore.

"Just trying to make you feel at home," I told Kristi.

She found everything intriguing. Catching a snapping turtle that would become soup, pulling in a dozen bluegills for a fish fry, harvesting onions from the garden, all this appealed to her practicality and thriftiness. The changing clouds reflected in the lake, the flowers, wild and domestic, the flash of bird colors in the trees pleased her eyes. She was as sensitive and aware as a wild thing in the woods, trying to miss nothing, remember everything. There was only one unharmonious note. On the second day of her visit she showed us a spot that itched on her wrist. I looked at it as did Alice. Alice looked at me and nodded. I reciprocated.

"What is it?" Kristi quavered.

We answered in unison.

"Poison ivy!"

Off we went to the local hospital's emergency room for a shot to prevent its spread. That was important. The next stop on Kristi's itinerary was Honolulu where she was to be bridesmaid at the wedding of a dear friend.

"What if it should appear on my face?" Kristi worried.

"You'll be quarantined and have to stay here for another week," I told her.

"But I can't be late," she wailed, "I already have my dress."

"Only kidding," I confessed, and, of course, I was.

It would have been nice to have kept her around but she left on schedule with a clear complexion and was probably more beautiful than the bride.

A later gift from Kristi, was Alison Chew, another Singapore girl. Somehow, in seeking an American education, Alison had settled for a stint at Southwestern Michigan University, near

Dowagiac, Michigan. One day she called us from that college, which, literally, sits in a cornfield. It's sort of all by itself, far from any metropolis and even a good distance from downtown Dowagiac. The voice that spoke to us was forlorn.

"Kristi Koh said to call you," it said, with unmistakable Oriental intonation, "I have brought you a gift she sent."

So, the next weekend we drove over and met Alison. No wonder she had sounded forlorn. The school had no real provision for international students. There was no campus housing. This lovely, little Chinese girl was living in a boarding house.

"How do you like American food?" we asked her, somewhere along the line.

"Potatoes," she said, and shrugged. "I do not care for potatoes, three times a day."

That was the menu being provided by her penurious landlady.

So we went to dinner at the local restaurant and she ate ravenously.

Before we left that day we promised to see about getting her transferred to Michigan State University, where I worked and where international students were both welcome and understood. By the following semester she was in residence on the Lansing campus, and an occasional week-ender at Aurohn Lake.

After a year she transferred to New York University for her M.B.A., but came back whenever she had vacations. Now she works in San Francisco but still returns, when possible, to visit what she considers her "American home."

She loves Alice's cooking, even the potatoes.

We have also enjoyed participating in chairman Deng Xiaoping's westernization of the Peoples' Republic of China. As that vast country moves to take its place in the modern world some of its citizens come to Michigan State University. One such is our friend, Hairong Li, of Beijing University. He is studying consumer research methodology. Because I've so enjoyed my association with the Chinese I found his office and introduced myself and, before you know it, I invited him to the farm.

His first reaction to our 153 acres was almost disbelief.

"All yours?" he said. His hand swept in a half-circle, tracing the horizon line.

"Yes," I told him. "Everything you see, the woods, the pasture, the lake."

"So much," he said, "So much for one man."

It's true. What seems simple enough to us is a matter of amazement for those to whom any sort of ownership is beyond reach. Later, Hairong brought his lovely wife, Ying, to Lansing. With considerable courage he then learned to drive a car, got a driver's license and, somehow, bought a 1984 Dodge Omni. He's in his mid-thirties, his only transportation at home was a bicycle, and, suddenly, he's driving through downtown Detroit, or crossing Mackinac Bridge on his way to Sault Ste. Marie.

Each man makes his own miracle.

One definition of cosmopolitan is "belonging to the whole world." Based on that, we know of no couple more fully cosmopolitan than Alan and Jan Croll. From childhoods in Rhodesia and Kenya to residence on Long Island, life in the Kalahari desert, and time in Canada, their paths eventually took them to England and then on to Singapore.

They have property on the tiny Isle of Man and now have retired there. On holidays they have hiked over Crete and other Greek Isles which they love. To our delight, one vacation time they decided to add Aurohn Lake to a vacation itinerary that already included San Francisco, the Redwoods, Salt Lake City, Yellowstone, Jackson Hole and the Grand Tetons, Chicago and, after us, New Orleans.

They arrived by Amtrak at Battle Creek, just eighteen miles away. Both were bouncy, ebullient, pleased with everything they had seen. It was Jan's first experience in the New World and she was liking it all immensely. She paints, as does Alan, and they see things as artists. For the week they were with us they hiked, sketched, and were out from first light until dusk. Much as he likes painting, Alan's grand passion is sailing. He races in regattas in the South China sea and the Straits of Malacca. He crews sleek, long vessels that cut the water like a shark's fin. When we worked together, out East, he would wax eloquent about the joys of yachtsmanship.

Feeling that he might welcome a bit of boating during their stay, I made appropriate preparations. Some years previously Kool cigarettes had offered an amazing premium. For two dozen package wrappers and around $100, you could get a sailboat. The shallow hull is fibreglass and the polyethelene sail, unfurled, is a giant Kool package. My interest in obtaining the craft had been born during a cruise of the Virgin Islands on a ninety-foot ketch.

I admired the smart seamanship of the captain and his wife and ached to emulate it. So I bought the tiny twelve-footer. The day it arrived, with instruction book in hand, I ventured forth against the wind, which promptly blew me backwards right down to the dam. Alice brought the rowboat and towed me back to the dock. Gradually the secrets of tacking and coming about were revealed and, eventually, though awkwardly, I could negotiate the length of the lake. That accomplished, the Kool Craft had gone into storage on some rafters in the garage, where it reposed until the Crolls came. Alan, bless his heart, didn't laugh at it.

On a perfectly gorgeous morning, complete with sapphire sky, powder puff clouds, wind-dappled water, he and Jan set sail. What a joy it was to watch them swooping, turning, skimming as his skill transformed the tiny boat into an American Cup champion. The green sail glinted in the sunlight, bellied out proudly and Al waved nonchalantly as they passed. For me, it was the high point of a nigh perfect week.

In our living room we have a wall devoted to paintings of places we've been as portrayed by artists we know. There's a black-and-white etching of sailboats off Singapore that Jan Croll sent at Christmas. Nearby, an oil painted view of an arm of Sydney Harbor as it appeared from our Northbridge house bears Sheila Murray's name. Ismail Mustam of Kuala Lumpur, who created the batik for our drapes, also gave us an impressionist picture of palm trees and sunlight in Malaysia. There's an ochre sky and seascape, broken by the lacework of a Kelong, or fishtrap. It epitomizes an oriental harbor and was created by a petite Sri Lankan lady, Daisy Campbell.

Together, these pictures recall a glorious time in our lives. Now, when friends from faraway places come here, we hope they find beautiful paintings to hang in their minds and memories.

Their visits mean a lot to us. Only Alice knows how much.

ALICE:

True.

I remember a day a dozen or so years ago. Things weren't going well. The tractor had broken down, skies were gray and rainy, nothing could cheer up my disconsolate husband. He paced about, muttering just loud enough for me to hear:

"What am I doing here at the end of a dirt road on a farm? I'm no farmer. I need people. I need intellectual stimulation."

I tried reassurance, but Ken raved on:

"What do you see as our life here? Me trying to fix machines that won't run? You weeding and canning? The two of us traveling ten miles on Saturday night to see a movie if we aren't snowed in? Tell me . . . what do you see?"

From somewhere an answer came to me and I used it.

"I see people from all over the world coming to visit us here."

Isn't it miraculous how the prediction came true?

16

Grandpa's Farm

KEN:

THERE IS a splendid Currier and Ives picture evoked by that lovely, old lyric:

"Over the river and through the wood
To grandfather's house we go."

In the mind's eye we see the arrival. Shouting children running up the steps to be embraced by the kindly, silver-haired couple awaiting them. Chestnuts roasting by an open fire. A huge, home-grown Christmas tree twinkling in the parlor and a golden-brown turkey oozing juices in the oven. Inside, all is warmth, coziness, comfort. Outside there are hills for sledding, trails for walking, icy ponds for skating.

If ever there was a vision to be savored and preserved it's that idyllic home of the old folks where young folks find love and fun and adventure. Lucky the family where it is more than a fantasy based on a traditional ditty. Lucky our family has been. Our son, Jeff, and daughter, Jan, grew up anticipating each summer's visit to the farm in Pennsylvania. There, Grandfather Guseman boosted them to the back of Dudejems, the patient pinto cow-pony, showed them how milk can be squirted from a cow's teat into a bucket, built a pond where they could watch the goldfish. They climbed in fragrant haymows, petted calves and laughed at baby pigs.

Their grandmother baked incomparable apple pies, and showed them old family albums, and played chinese checkers. Some years, we drove the 500 miles over the hills and through the woods and were on hand for Thanksgiving dinner. Aunts and uncles and cousins crowded around a groaning table, and it was a family occasion as well as a feast.

During the years that our kids were growing up in the city, it never occurred to us that we might, someday, become, to our grandchildren, the old folks on the farm.

But, providentially, that dream we never had, has come true. For our five grandchildren "Grandpa's farm" is a palpable, constant and beloved reality. Should everything here vanish tomorrow, the Currier and Ives image of what it once was, will be engraved in the minds of Sean and Keeley Geary, the memories of Wiley, Adam and, the youngest, Theodore Llewelyn Jones.

Sean, the oldest, has always been the most venturesome, not because of his age but because of his nature. On a summer's day, when the family arrives, he is out of the car door and down to the lake's edge after a hurried "Hi." He grabs a net, on the run, and we watch him from a window. His eyes are unbelievably sharp. He spots two dots bulging from a patch of green algae. Woosh goes the net and a big bullfrog is enmeshed and brought to bucket. Now Sean crouches on the dock and peers at the edge of the island twenty feet away. He rises and stalks something, then disappears. Those of us watching are diverted, forget about him. Ten minutes later the door flies open and he's in the room, breathless, flushed, eager.

"I can't get him," he pants, "The snake won't let him go."

"Can't get what?" his mother, our daughter, Jan asks.

"The frog," Sean explains, "The snake won't let him go."

"Snake?" Jeff Geary, the concerned father is on his feet and moving. Sean is with him and they are off and running down the hill, the rest of us following. By the time we're all at the lake Sean is pointing.

"There, see!"

We see, all right. A disconsolate frog, already a third swallowed, croaks in anguish. His legs have disappeared down the throat of a large water snake who hasn't sufficient power to haul the unfortunate amphibian away.

Sean had complicated the situation by grabbing the other end of the croaker and trying to remove him from the serpentine swallow. It was an impasse so, naturally, the boy had come for aid and assistance.

"It's the snake's dinner," Jeff explained. "He needs the frog more than you do."

Keeley started to cry.

"The poor frog," she sobbed.

"We're going back to the house," Jan said firmly.

Alice agreed and the three ladies trotted back up the hill.

Sean reached down and grabbed his end of the frog. The snake thrashed about but was in no position to retaliate, his jaws being otherwise occupied.

"Why don't you give him a break," suggested Jeff.

"He's not giving the frog a break," replied Sean, reasonably.

"It's amazing that he'd tackle such a big frog," I pointed out. "Think he can actually get it all down?"

Sean released his hold. We watched. The snake, now without competition, set about engulfing his interrupted meal. Slowly, inevitably, with a rather resigned look Sean's erstwhile trophy disappeared. The boy watched without a word. The meal completed, visible as a large lump within his skin, the victor then wriggle-waddled into a hiding place to await digestion.

"What did you think of that?" I asked.

"Neat," was Sean's evaluation.

The Gearys seldom leave without a few jars and converted

plastic milk jugs from Grandma's inexhaustible supply. She knows Sean will need them for the fauna he finds on the farm.

He is growing up. He has, in fact, reached an age of independence that must be honored. He now explores in the rowboat without adult companionship. One day he had inveigled his parents into such an expedition and was gone for a worrisome length of time. Nobody seemed much concerned except me.

"He'll be fine," said Jan, offhandedly, as I voiced concern.

"Right," seconded Jeff. "He likes to get off on his own."

Even Alice was indifferent to the lad's peril, out there on the lake, up around the bend, out of sight.

I decided to go rabbit hunting, even though the season had been over for a month. Arming myself with a twenty-gauge I set forth and just happened to wander up into a little woods near the bend where Sean had disappeared an hour earlier. I walked stealthily, so that I wouldn't startle any out-of-season rabbits. I stopped and listened.

"You just wait a minute," I heard Sean's voice. "Open your mouth so I can put you on the stringer."

Like any experienced fisherman, he was talking to his catch. I sat down, grinning as the monologue continued. The splash of his lure hitting the water, the muttered "C'mon fish, bite," the sound of the reel winding in, it was all music to an old angler's ears. After a while I got up, stomped, coughed and crashed through the brush to a place where the boat was in view.

"Hi, Grandpa, what are you doing?" said grandson.

"Rabbit hunting," lied Grandpa, "How about a ride back to the house?"

"Sure," agreed Sean, "If you'll row. I'm tired from catching fish."

He hauled his stringer out of the water. Four nice-sized bass, a couple of crappie and a big sunfish flopped and glistened in the afternoon sunlight.

"Nice catch." was my accolade.

"I'll help clean them," said Isaac Walton, "Then mom can cook them when we go home."

Keeley has her own routines. She is a beauty lover. She doesn't walk down the hill, she dances. She curtsies to the pussy willow tree, and talks to the wildflowers. To her, there are no weeds, only lovely blossoms. She coaxes Grandma to go for a walk and they make bouquets of Queen Anne's lace, goldenrod, dandelions, and Indian paintbrush. Alice places them, carefully, in small vases and, even after the Gearys are gone, Keeley's image remains, enshrined for a day, until the blossoms wilt.

On hot summer days, the waterfront fascinates her. She spends hours paddling in an innertube, wading, making sand structures, talking, often, to an invisible companion who also seems to like things acquatic. She performs water ballets, and sometimes parades as Miss America in an old evening gown of her mother's. Her own imagination supplies all the audience and applause she needs.

Like any younger sister she feels the urge to emulate her brother. At four, for instance, having watched Sean handle a fishing rod, she announced that she wished to do likewise.

"Show her how, Grandpa." directed my daughter.

For just such occasions we have a kid-sized rod and reel. Keeley watched and listened raptly as I explained how it worked and was eager to try for herself. Her tiny thumb pressed the reel release button firmly, but she couldn't quite coordinate the forward fling of the rod with the raising of the thumb. She handed the rig back to me.

"Grandpa do it," she directed.

I threw the line out, handed the rod back to her. She reeled in slowly. Nothing nibbled or struck so we tried again.

This time she reeled some of the line in and then stopped.

"I'll fish here," Keeley informed me.

For a while I let her. Then, in my infinite wisdom, I informed her that the fish were probably farther out toward the middle of the lake and she should let Grandpa cast for her again.

She shook her head, wisely, and explained.

"No," she said, "It's better to fish here." She pointed down into the clear, motionless water. "Here I can catch clouds."

Then I saw what she saw. Great, fluffy, cumulus clouds, reflected in the water, drifted up to her line, were hooked, landed and captured in Keeley's creel.

Fantasy, on a sweet summer's day, can be more fun than fishing.

When vacation time arrives at the Jeff Jones household some hundred-and-twenty-five miles away, Wiley, our son's oldest son, has plans. He feels that, for him, a week at Grandpa's farm is his right. It's a chance to get away from younger brothers who cling, and parents who direct, and to be king of the roost for a while. Sometimes, when business takes me to the city I drive by to pick him up. Bag packed, he's ready to go the minute I arrive and is impatient with motherly admonitions to "do what Grandma and Grandpa tell you to."

Adam, his nearest sibling, watches wistfully as we head for the car and wonders, aloud, how soon he'll be old enough for his own week away. Like all mothers, Claudia wishes her eldest showed a little more reluctance to leave home, but she's glad for him.

Our conversation is desultory as we drone along the freeway. I point out the state capitol building, dome lit in the distance.

"I know," he says, "That's where the Boss lives."

That's how he sees our Governor.

He asks a couple of questions and my answers about the workings of the legislature are too long, too complex. I gently lower his seat back so he can sleep comfortably. He wakes up when we hit the bumpy gravel road close to home, sits forward.

"Look, Grandpa, look!"

A deer's eyes glow at the roadside, caught in the glare of the headlights. The animal steps daintily in front of us as I brake to a stop, then trots a few yards, turns, and is off into the brush.

"Boy," Wiley says, "Wait 'til I tell Adam about *that*."

The front porch lights are on as we dip over the hill and Grandma is waiting for her boy. Of course he's hungry enough for cookies, and with a nap behind him, not too anxious for bed. It's late by the time he's tucked in and early, too early, when I'm roused the next morning.

"Hi Grandpa," Wiley says, "Is it time to feed the cows yet?"

It's one of the weekends when it's my turn to hay the beef cattle and he knows it. Actually, it's about two hours earlier than necessary, but I roll out and get dressed. Alice is already in the kitchen and cornmeal cakes, syrup and sausage are ready and waiting by the time I'm dressed. After breakfast we bundle up against the cold. Bandit, the bossy pup, precedes us to the garage, takes his post on the seatback the instant I open the pickup's door.

"Can I ride in back?" asks Wiley. Kids seem to prefer the hard, corrugated surface of a truck bed to the upholstered comfort of the seat.

"Too cold," I tell him, "Get up here with me and Bandit."

He climbs in, and we head for the barn. A rabbit zig-zags frantically across the road and Wiley's thumb and forefinger become a pistol.

"Got him," he exclaims.

The unaware rabbit streaks away, unscathed.

When we get to the gate that opens into the upper pasture, Wiley climbs down, unlocks it and swings it back, holding it as I drive through. He closes it, then hops back aboard, hangs the keys on the dash where they belong, all without a word. He knows the drill. So do the cattle. This time of the year the coming of the truck means mealtime and they moo, softly, in anticipation. My grandson gets out, not so boldly now. He's strange to the cattle and they eye him suspiciously. He's glad when we're inside the barn.

"That Evergreen Freestate (he knows the bull's name) is *big*."

We climb the ladder to the hayloft. It's early in the season and bales are stacked twenty feet high. One side is stair-stepped enough for me to climb to the top. Long-legged Wiley makes it, too. He watches as I pitch bales to the floor. Then he shoves one to the edge of the pile, pushes it over. It lands with a satisfying thud. Later, at ground level, he wrestles the big rectangles of alfalfa to the doorway where I can grab them and take them to the feeders. He's reluctant to get in the crowd of cows as they push for position. They weigh 800 pounds to his 100 and his circumspection is understandable.

"Wiley was a big help at the barn," I tell Alice when we're back in the house.

"I'll bet he was," she responds.

Wiley glows.

When he comes for his summer time with us Grandma's golf cart is the preferred means of transportation. It's an ancient, gas-powered vehicle that binder twine and boxes have converted into a mini-truck. It saves a lot of steps to mailbox, garden and dam. The operation is simple, a footpedal accelerator and brake, a tiller to steer it.

Having seen youngsters no older than Wiley and Sean operate huge tractors on nearby farms, we've decided to let our grandsons get early driver's training on the golf cart. It's nice to see Wiley, after helping his grandmother harvest tomatoes, squash, broccoli, and beans, chugging up the hill to deliver them to the house.

Best are those special days when all of them are on the premises. They split off into cousinly couples. The "big boys," Sean Geary and Wiley Jones are absolutely unpredictable. They'll spend a little time in the fort Grandma helped them build in the gully west of the house, repairing and fixing. A clamber up the big ash tree behind the garden shed will follow. There's a tree house there that Sean and Jeff Geary hammered into place one busy weekend and it needs a check.

Those things attended to, the boys will be off on invented errands and imagined missions. Often they take along peanut butter sandwiches and homemade cookies commandeered from Grandma's kitchen. Once they dragged a decrepit red wagon across the dam and a good half-mile up into the woods. They couldn't recall what they had intended to bring back but they were glad of my help in getting the wagon home again.

"I think we were going to get apples," Sean recalled as we

headed up the hill.

"They won't be ripe for another two months." It seemed to me they should know that.

"Maybe it was kindling wood," Wiley suggested.

"Probably." We were close enough to see the mothers standing on the back deck.

"They're fine." I shouted.

My reconnaisance had been the result of expressed maternal concern after the boys had been gone for a couple of hours.

"They were up in the woods after kindling."

At six, Jan's girl, Keeley, and Claudia's Adam are really a picture as they trot off together, often hand-in-hand. The limit of their range is the sandpit, a vein of fine, brown sand just below the dam. There, with some beat-up toy trucks, they can build cities and roads. Just adjacent are blackberry bushes and, in season, they can pick their own refreshments. How long their idyllic relationship will last is anybody's guess but at six they are the perfect pair, never arguing, content in each other's companionship.

Sometimes, when it's raining, they persuade Grandma to make playdough. Kneading, coloring, shaping it with cookie cutters is fun, but messy. Once, Adam called from Detroit for the recipe. He said his mother didn't know how to make it. Claudia doesn't really want to learn.

Curious and forthright, Adam always says exactly what he thinks. Last summer he was trying to get Alice to swing on a rope and she protested that she was too old.

"I know, Grandma," Adam sympathized, "I can tell by your neck."

The youngest of all, Tiny Ted, at two, confines his explorations to our house. Four distinct levels, and his new found skill in negotiating stairways, make it a veritable continent to be discovered. There is the gun room where a glowing stove is not to be approached and books on shelves are no-nos. Three steps up lead to the big living room and the fascination of the Toy Box.

This capacious space, built into a window ledge, is the repository of a helter-skelter collection of playthings accumulated over the years. There are quacking ducks-on-wheels, building blocks, beads, buckets, buttons, cars, trucks, tanks, dolls, hand puppets, horns, harmonicas, trays, dishes, an endless collection of things to be considered.

Ted usually carries a few of these things along as he goes to the toy electric organ in one corner and sounds a few tentative notes. Then it's up some more stairs and into the dining room where the candy jar is. Look up expectantly and a kind adult may slip you a piece. Then the kitchen, where Grandma spends so much time, and the breakfast room, where there's a table with paper and crayolas for a few minutes of scribbling. Finally, there's the guest bedroom and a big bed for naps, but there's many a circuit to be made before it's time for that.

Christmas, of course, is special. The Scotch pines planted when first we came have supplied us with ten foot trees for the past several years. Each year one towers from floor level, up past the bedroom balcony and the angel at the top reaches for the ceiling. Near the base is Lionelville station at one end of an oval of track, and Jones Junction at the other. Between them runs Train Number 8, the standard-gauge Lionel that brightened my Christmas morning in 1927. Now the hands on the transformer are Sean's and Wiley's, Adam's and Keeley's and, tentatively, Ted's. They watch raptly as it circles, lights on the engine and in the passenger cars, glowing in the darkened room. Above them the colored tree bulbs are imaginary stars, and the fire crackling in the fireplace is the sun in a small universe. Once, we photographed Number 8 and memorialized it with a Christmas card verse:

It's never late, not Number 8, the local Lionel.
On Christmas Eve, you'd better believe, it will weave its magic spell.
Round and round, with whistle's sound, it circles each year's tree,
Just as alive at fifty-five as it was at two or three.
And young eyes flash to watch its dash
And young hands make it run
And young hearts lift at song and gift and Yuletide's feast and fun.

That's the way it was, in December, when the family came to the farm. Outside the snow drifted down and clothed the pines in white.

It's a Currier and Ives print to hang in the memories of Sean and Keeley, Wiley, Adam and Theodore.

Sometimes we wonder about how they will recall it all when they are our age. Chances are that the farm will have long since passed out of family hands, at least so it seems now. Our kids are both devoted urbanites. They view our home as a wonderful place to visit, but no one seems interested in the work it takes to keep it all running. It's kind of a family Disneyland. There are boats to row and tractors to ride and calves to watch. There's fishing, and flowers and fun all around. Here's how Keeley saw it just before her eighth birthday? We were in town and watching a baseball game in which her brother was playing and she was sitting beside me in the bleachers. Suddenly, without preface, she said, softly:

"Grandpa, you've got it *all*.

"You've got your very own lake.

"You've got a mansion.

"You've got your own forest.

"Grandpa, you've got it *all*."

When I'm mowing or hoeing, when Alice is weeding or planting, those are nice words to have tucked away. Or, when, occasionally, some twinge of doubt assails me as to whether I should have left the wild and wonderful advertising agency world as early as I did, they reassure me.

In the meantime, the years streak by and the boys are young men. Jeff Jones and Wiley load the shotguns and shoot trap together. Jeff Geary and Sean take the chainsaw and cut a load of firewood. Keeley helps with dinner in the kitchen. Adam is off fishing by himself. Even Teddy is old enough to find his own fun with the red wagon and toy bulldozer out in the garage.

They are all writing new chapters in the story of Grandpa's Farm.

17

Owners of All Outdoors

KEN:

GRANTED, we have surveys and deeds that give us title to this acreage. Our house, outbuildings and barn attest to our determination to reside here. Our cattle are tenants, too.

But a little observation, day or night, winter or summer, will clue you in on the real owners, who staked their claim here long ago. When it was forest land, they watched the Potawatamie Indians tread the narrow trails. They were on hand when the first owner of the farm, a veteran of the Black Hawk War, claimed the land that had been given him as a bonus. They've seen steam engines replace horse-drawn plows and, in turn, give way to cleat-wheeled tractors. Everything changes, but the original residents linger. Despite hunting, trapping, feral cats and predator dogs, they dig dens, build nests, breed, grow and multiply. They are, after all, better neighbors to us than we are to them. Birds, beasts and bugs we call them and they are beyond counting. We're acquainted with just a few.

Rabbits, of course, those heroes of Watership Downs,

abound here. Their presence is most apparent during hard winter. When the snow is drifted two and three feet deep the bunnies become adjacent-to-the-house pets. They nibble the branches of our ornamental shrubs, devour the leaves of creeping cover plants, crouch under junipers and pfitzer bushes, huddle along the warm foundations. They pound out a hardened path through the snow from nearby gullies to our doorsteps. Rabbit pellets are everywhere. Sometimes Alice gets aggravated at their depradations and then I try to hunt or trap them.

Box traps capture a couple who venture in to try a succulent apple or carrot. But they must communicate because after two or three unfortunates are corralled, the rest avoid the bait. As for around-the-house hunting, it is as short-lived. Bag a bunny and all his buddies become phantoms. They forage when it's pitch dark, or by the light of the moon. At the crack of dawn, or the sound of a door opening they disappear as magically as they materialize from a magician's hat. Whoever said dumb didn't know bunnies.

In the spring you'll see tiny and incredibly cute young rabbits along the roadside. Enjoy them for a while. Come summer they all turn large, voracious and make a beeline for tender, growing things in the garden.

It takes all their cunning, speed and fecundity to survive. Once I saw a Cooper's Hawk follow one right into a stand of brush, maneuver, plunge and strike before the rabbit could hit a hole. Often, in the winter, you'll find a bunch of hair and blood and the marks of an owl's wings in the snow. Near a fox's den there are bunny bones and wandering cats can decimate a nest of young ones in a matter of moments.

One heartless reason I applaud their survival. The four or five rabbits I manage to snare or shoot each winter are absolutey delicious.

Also fair game is the fox squirrel. They do nothing to incur our wrath and it's only their succulence that brings them down and into our larder. That and the fun of hunting them. Playford Van Sickle, our brother-in-law, drives 1,000 miles round-trip, every year, to be here during squirrel season. He's out at daybreak, in at dark, and four or five times a day we'll hear his old pump shotgun roar. He's happy with the day's bag, we're happy with the squirrel stew. The real winners are Alice and Ina who have their annual, treasured, sisterly visit while the menfolk stalk the bushytail. Again, because there is minimum hunting pressure in our woods, the population stays stable.

Not for food, but for fur, do some of the other occupants of the place fall victim to man. Once the lake was built and aquatic plants began to flourish, in moved the muskrats. With as many as a dozen young to a litter, and three litters a year, their tribe increased with incredible rapidity. So did the holes in the banks of the lake. When evidence of their digging appeared on the face of the dam I was understandably worried and made a few amateurish and desultory attempts at trapping. When, to place the trap, you must plunge your arm to the elbow in frigid water it dampens enthusiasm for the pursuit. Or catch a couple of fingers in a trap just once and see how interest flags. It was with real pleasure that I heard these words from Marty:

"Would you mind if I set some 'rat traps in your lake?"

In a good winter he'll take one hundred pelts. Yet, by spring, we'll again see the neat V-shaped wakes in the water as muskrats build and supply their houses. They are interesting neighbors and live here at their own risk. Worse for them than any trapper, is the bloodthirsty mink that follows muskrat populations from lake to lake, stream to stream. We've seen their sleek and sinuous forms undulating across the dock, plunging into the water. Their pelts bring as much as thirty dollars (a muskrat's four or five) so Marty makes special sets to catch them.

"It pays two ways," he says, "What we get for the mink plus all the muskrat we save for next year's trapping."

Raccoons are fun to watch. They'll crouch at the lake's edge, intent on watching the water, grabbing for crayfish, fast as a boxer's jab. Mostly nocturnal, they'll occasionally shinny up our back deck's supports and try for the suet that hangs there for the birds. They're great for garden corn, too and you'll find ears they've husked and eaten still on bent stalks.

Fair game for hunters and trappers, the coons lead harried lives from October until February. For property owners with conservationist tendencies, they can cause a peculiar problem. One moonlit October midnight we had just retired. Then we heard the hounds. I sat up in bed.

"What is it? What's the matter?" asked Alice.

"They're on our place," I said. "Sounds like right across the lake."

"They're probably miles away," she said, "go to sleep."

The belling continued, insistently for another forty minutes.

"Something's treed," I persisted. "And it's in our woods."

Now custom directs that a hunter may follow his hounds across posted land, which ours is. But he's to leave his guns behind, recover his dogs and vacate promptly. That's what custom directs but few hunters follow. More likely, the inveterate night nimrod will get permission to hunt one place and then go wherever the hounds run, take the game and be gone. Not on this ground, not tonight, I decided. By the time a wool shirt and blue jeans covered my pajamas and the socks and shoes joined them, Alice was ready with her pronouncement.

"You're crazy," she pronounced.

The Jeep truck's lights cut a yellow swath through the mist as it bounced its way toward the fence corner where the baying continued. Two flashlights came bobbing towards the vehicle and then I could see two men in raingear. The hounds preceded them.

"What's your name," I yelled.

Taken unawares, the leading man told me his. I bellowed the same question at the other guy and he answered, too.

"Get the hell off this property," was my cordial follow-up, "and if I ever catch you here again you'll hear from the sheriff."

"We got permission," grumbled one shadowy figure.

"Who from?"

"Charlie Tobias."

Charlie had gone to a happier hunting ground the year before.

I looked at the guns they were carrying, considered the place and the hour and discretion seemed like a good idea. So I didn't call him a liar. Instead I allowed as how he'd probably made a mistake, showed him where Charlie's property ended and mine began. The men and the dogs disappeared. An old hunting adage came to mind. Always leave a cornered creature a way out if you don't want to get bit. Poachers are a lawless, dangerous breed. Whether these were deliberate poachers or just a couple of over-enthused coon hunters, I'll never know. But they certainly haven't been back.

Real trappers, as well as landowners, aren't too happy about coon hunters. The shooting season starts nearly a month before traps can be set. Most hunters are simply after sport. To the trappers a good pelt means thirty dollars.

By limiting trapping and keeping hunting to one or two nights a year we're keeping quite a few coons as neighbors.

Two members of the local fauna are extremely unpopular with trappers. One is the skunk, that fearless little woods pussy. A tiny one walked through our pasture. The cows saw it. One young heifer went to investigate. The skunk discouraged her curiosity in the only way he knew. She was an outcast from the rest of the herd for a week. Wherever she went, they didn't.

The other trapper's anathema is the lowly possum. This nosy, greedy creature is always on the prowl for food; and any bait seems to attract him. He springs the snares set for other crea-tures and is killed and cast aside. Yet, the species flourishes and more of them seem to perish on the county roads and highways than do in the woods. It's true, most of them do "play possum" if you surprise them and they can't waddle away. They curl up, stiffen and hold the pose even if poked and prodded. Pick them up by the tail, if you want to, but keep your hands away from the needle sharp teeth.

Once, inadvertently, a badger was trapped and killed. His claws were most impressive and you could believe that he can dig almost as fast as a man can walk. A protected species, he's rare enough and I have yet to see one in the woods, although we've found their dens.

Most elusive and canniest of the fur bearers is the fox. He is an orange streak tearing across the pasture, bushy tail streaming behind him. He might be glimpsed when you are still-hunting in the woods, skulking along in his endless search for food. If you're very lucky you might see a vixen and her pups near a den entrance scuffling in the warm sunlight. Fox trapping seems to be an art practiced and understood by few. Most trappers don't have the time and patience required. One trace of human scent, one change in the accustomed landscape and foxes take a wide detour. Pelts sell for as much as $50 or $60, but the real prize is simply being smart enough to catch wily Renard.

Although his fur is of little value, the hardy groundhog comes in for his share of attention. He's a remarkable underground engineer, and his subterranean home requires several entrances. Usually they turn out to be holes in the hayfield, places to turn ankles, jar machinery and provide Mr. Woodchuck with endless meals of alfalfa. One enterprising member of the family wanted a dry home so his tunnel emerged in the barn and threatened to undercut a support pole. So hunting and trapping these inhabitants is for our own protection. With borrowed traps I took three from the barn den. A fourth was seen up in an adjacent mulberry tree enjoying the sweet fruit. Notified by a neighbor, I hiked up with a .22 rifle and eliminated him. Then we filled in the barn tunnel with rocks and dirt and that seems to be that.

Not so successful was Marty's campaign against a hayfield encroacher. He set smoke bombs, designed for the purpose, in an entrance to the tunnel and, rifle at the ready, watched what he assumed to be the exit. Apparently there was yet a third opening because no groundhog, coughing and choking, ever appeared.

Chipmunks, moles, voles, field mice, red squirrels, all are to be seen around the place. Find a spot almost anywhere, sit down, sit still and quiet, and an amazing number of woodland travelers will pass in review. Most exciting is the deer. Whether it's an antlered buck in hunting season, or a doe and fawn in summertime, the sight of them stirs the senses. Generations of fear is in the careful tread, the constant alertness, twitching ear and flared nostril. As large as they are, these animals can materialize within a dozen feet of you like they had risen from the forest floor. One small move, or a turn of the wind so your scent reaches them, and up go the tails, white flags of warning. There's a cough of alarm, a huge bound and the woods are suddenly empty and still.

During the ninety days when bow hunters, muzzle-loader aficionados, and shotgun toters cruise the country in search of venison, how the herd seems to shrink! Down in the swamps and potholes, under fallen trees or in grapevine thickets the deer lie still as death. Only when the sun is down do they rise and move tentatively, watchfully, towards food and water.

It's at dusk and dawn that the wise hunter is in the woods, sitting like a statue, hoping to see his quarry before he himself is discovered because of a tiny move, a twig's cracking, a wayward wind shift. Like an illusion, almost, a big, six-point buck is suddenly in sight and range. The heart pounds but the gun comes up, steadies, roars. A whirl and leap and now the heart sinks in disappointment. Walk carefully to the place where the target stood. Find blood and hair and take the trail, eyes straining for flecks of red. There he is, down and dead. Then, the ritual of field dressing, dragging the hundred and fifty pounds to an open spot, getting truck or tractor for the ride home. Venison chops, venison roasts of fine flavor come from a quickly-killed, promptly dressed animal. He's as much a part of our annual protein crop as is the beef we butcher.

One month after the last, laggard bow hunter has gone, eight weeks after the gun season, four days into a major winter blizzard we see them.

Seventeen deer cross the ice of the lake headed into a cornfield where stalks still stand. Our efforts are providing the forage that will sustain them until spring and the arrival of the fawns.

One fall morning, after we had driven in from the city and spent a comfortable night in the mobile home that was then our shelter, we had an incomparable thrill. Something, some sound awakened me. I listened, then nudged Alice awake. She listened, too. Then I opened the drapes and we looked at the lake.

Ducks, hundreds of ducks, covered it. Their lengthy morning conversations were what we had overheard. They were Golden-eyes, in transit, headed south. The flocks arrived, faithfully, for several years, then, apparently their routing changed and we've never seen wildfowl in such numbers again. But we do have our regulars. Wood ducks, in their Harlequin dress, are the most beautiful of all. For years they have nested in the boxes we nailed to old tree stumps out in the lake. Now we've added some luxury fibreglass apartments designed by Duck's Unlimited. All nests are occupied in the summer. In the fall the woodies return regularly to a small peninsula with two oak trees on it. Acorns are their favorite food. During my brother-in-law's hunting stay, he might take a few for the table and for the feathers that fly-tying friends crave.

Still, the tribe increases.

Usually a couple of families of mallards spend the summer here and it's a joy to see the convoys of ducklings crossing from cove to cove. Not such a joy is the attrition as snapping turtles systematically follow and pull under a duckling a day, until only one or two out of ten are left to grow and fly. Those that do mature are usually gone by October and so avoid the arrival of hunting days.

Then there are the Canadians, the great black, gray and white geese whose cry still sends chills down the spine. They are the percursors of seasons, dragging winter southward hitched to their high-flying V's, and heralding spring as they honk northward to the country that gave them their name.

One spring a single pair found our place good and stayed to nest and multiply. Now four or five generations linger with us from April to December and as many as fifty goslings perform their solo flights as we watch them in late summer. This year, an oddity appears. A dazzling, white snow goose has somehow joined our little flock of black and gray Canadians. They seem quite unaware of the difference and he or she seems to be happily paired with a smaller partner. Apparently integration comes easy to geese.

If the flock is here for hunting season we might bag one or two. We always try to take those that are young and unattached so as not to cause sorrow to a surviving mate among these monagamous birds. If you have ever heard a bereaved goose moan, seen it fly back day after day in search of the lost one, you would understand.

The marshy wetlands are wonderful habitat for other winged neighbors. Most spectacular is the long-legged great blue heron. Their slow, dignified flight into the top of a dead tree is something to watch.

The legs and talons reach out, grasp a limb and sort of pull the big body into an upright position. From this vantage point the bird observes. Somehow he seems to pick a shoreline spot to which he moves. Then, in the shallows, he stands motionless until a fish comes in range. The serpentine neck uncoils, the fearsome beak grabs and pierces, and dinner has been served. Once, when I was fly-fishing along the lake's edge and making as little noise as possible, I inadvertently moved to within ten feet of a Great Blue. Startled, he flew and I thought it was a disturbed angel. A seventy-inch wingspread is hard to imagine until one tip of it practically brushes your ear.

Sitting quietly in the rowboat you watch the traffic. A shitepoke or green heron, small cousin to the blue, rasps at you as he passes overhead. Two red-headed woodpeckers drum on a drowned tree at the margin of the lake. A kingfisher darts down and up with a flopping sunfish in its beak. Red-winged blackbirds buzz you if you float too close to nests in the cattails. Swallows dip to within an inch of the surface in pursuit of dragonflies. On a rare occasion an osprey arrives, to spend a week fishing.

Of late, a new and haunting cry drifts down from the sky. It's the sound of sandhill cranes, nesting nearby. Near extinction, once, they've staged a heartening comeback, and we occasionally glimpse one standing in a field, cinnamon brown, when young, and wearing a little red skullcap.

While the sun is hot, look for the most primordial of the lake creatures, the turtles. Painted terrapins, lined up like a chorus on a half-sunken log. Come close and they slide into the water like mermaids in an acquacade.

The surface is broken twenty feet from the boat and a fearsome beak emerges. It's the giant snapper, and you can see his jagged outline just below the surface. Those are the jaws that can drag a duck under or sever a finger.

To us, he's the hunted as well as the hunter. He's been caught on big hooks, baited and hung from floating jugs. He's been trapped in specially built traps. On land he's easy. Kick him over on his back, grab him by the tail, put him in a gunny sack. Why? Because he, for all his ugliness, makes a tasty dish. Turtle meat, dressed out, sells for $4.50 a pound.

While we're ruminating, the snout disappears and the object of our thoughts heads for the murky bottom. Close to shore there's a tenative *guruuunnnk*. Scan the lily pads and find the bulging eyes and white throat of a bullfrog. Once a year, in early June, Marty and I hunt this species. We start at dark, just when the mosquitos are busiest. Marty crouches in the boat's prow, shining a powerful, battery powered light. It picks up those eyes, that shining throat. Quietly we row close, Marty's hand shoots out, grabs, pulls the kicking frog aboard and we stuff him in a gunny sack. With twenty-five or thirty of his fellows he'll provide succulent frog legs for a future feast.

The sun goes down, the traffic slows, the residents roost. Then, suddenly, a big-bodied hoot owl floats out of the woods ready for his night's work. You row in to the dock, tie up and a screech owl cries like a baby somewhere out there. Then the air is still and the stars are out.

Songbirds are pure pleasure in the summertime. The music they make from June until October is ear pleasing and their flashing colors are something to watch. The orange and black of the oriole, bluebirds and indigo buntings like pieces of sky, brilliant yellow goldfinches, slashes of cardinal color, flamboyant scarlet tanagers weave in and out of thickets. Robins, harbingers of the thaw, bring the lawn to life as they search for early worms. Blackbirds, like deacons, patrol nearby.

Nests appear everywhere. Wrens build in their house in the grape arbor.

Killdeers, foolishly, build on the ground by the driveway, redbirds in the cedar by the front door. A fearless phoebe perches her nest on the fixture that holds a porch swing, so we stop using it and allow her peaceful brooding. One year the barn swallows found their usual place atop an old broken light fixture on the mobile home had disappeared. So, they moved inside the garage. That's not too great for car finishes but we allowed them lodging until their fledglings flew. Alice built some shelving outside the garage for future swallow housing.

The real suspense of the season is awaiting the arrival of the purple martins. Before we had any house of our own we bought a metal martin house on a ten foot pole and set it in concrete just north of the lake's edge. One summer passed with it untenanted. The second summer, in mid-April, on our son's birthday, the first scout arrived. He perched on the peak of the roof and sang his liquid, gurgling, lovely song. Then he flew away and we waited. Somewhere south he contacted his friends and brought them to our place with its dozen neat apartments and they moved in happily.

So it was for several years and then the neighborhood changed. Each year we take the house down, clean it good, and return it to the pole in early April. This time, two raffish English sparrows started carrying grass and straw into one shelter. After several days I took the house down and threw their trash out. They promptly started over. I plinked at them with a BB gun and they weren't too disconcerted. Finally I got the .22 out and did some serious shooting. Before another interloper arrived the martins showed up and took possession. Throughout their tenancy they continued to fight with the sparrows who tried to claim the several empty spaces. It concerned us. We love the martins not only for their wonderful warble and fancy flight but because they eat several thousand mosquitos a day. What bothers them, bothers us.

So, year in and year out, we continue a defensive campaign against those sparrows and some tree swallows who have designs on the highly desirable condominium reserved for their majesties, the purple martins.

There are other wars to be waged, in self-defense.

Chipmunks can play havoc around a house foundation. With trap and gun you reclaim the ground, close the tunnels, fill the holes. Ground hogs around a barn or outbuilding, or in a cultivated field are encroachers who must be trapped and destroyed. Appealing as they are, field mice can't be taken in as boarders and every fall the traps are set.

Perhaps our toughest campaigns have been against the persistent and prolific yellowjackets who take up residence in the eaves or under the shingles of our roof. Somehow, they find their way into the house and a few painful stings will activate a no-quarter effort. Sprays, putties, vacuum cleaners can keep them in check, but only the cold of winter finally defeats them.

When all the summer residents are gone, our winter responsibilities begin. As the days chill, the chickadees come closer to the house as do the goldfinches and juncos. Tree sparrows perch expectantly on the deck railing. We stock up on bird feed.

Sunflower seed and suet, thistle seed and ear corn, peanut butter and a concoction Alice makes of lard and bird seed. We get the feeders out of storage. There's an oversize mason jar that hangs like a tiny greenhouse. Chickadees walk right in and help themselves to sunflower seed. A big converted glass outdoor lamp shade holds a seed mix attractive to juncos, sparrows, and the despised starling. Ear corn is for cardinals and bluejays, suet in net bags for the downy woodpeckers, nuthatches and a big red-bellied woodpecker. The long, narrow thistle feeder is exclusively for finches. As winter builds, so does the traffic on the back deck. As many as fifty birds of nine different species will be busy stocking up on the eve of a blizzard. They have their own early warning system. Feathers fluffed out like overcoats they feed from first light until dark and bring us endless enjoyment when we are housebound. The 100 pounds of seed that it costs is a tiny price to pay.

How many thousands of flying, walking, crawling, wriggling, swimming, very animate beings share our farm? The bullfrogs who chant until the whole lake seems to pulsate; terrapins basking on logs in the August sunlight; dragon flies poised iridescently on water weeds, butterflies and humming birds stealing nectar from the flower garden, grackles strutting about, a box turtle lumbering along.

Busy, but never overcrowded, that's our place.

Sometimes it seems heartless to fill our larder at the expense of the creatures who share the accommodations. Professionals assure us that they are a "renewable resource" as long as we observe reasonable conservation measures.

We do.

Like the Potawatomies, after a brief stay, we'll be gone and, bar Armegeddon, the real owners of Aurohn Lake will still be acting out their dramas on this lovely stage.

18

Doubts, Dilemmas, and Decisions

KEN:

WHEN WE WERE weekend sojourners, neither of us had a moment's doubt about the wisdom of our bucolic buy. Hours at the lake were tonic and elixir, guaranteed to prepare mind and body for five days of office work and city hassling.

But after we made the Big Move and settled into a permanently different life style there began to be recurring questions about the wisdom of our decision. The first year was easy. Along with being Lord of the Manor I also set about becoming one of America's favorite novelists. Years of office discipline made it fairly easy for me to be at my desk by eight A.M., to roll a piece of blank paper into the IBM Selectric, and to spin a web of words until lunch time. Afternoons were scheduled for out-of-doors and all the strange new jobs that came with the place.

Alice, of course, never had any problem filling her hours in the country. Eight months of the year there is always a little weeding to do, a posy to plant, a branch to trim. Courting birds are better to watch than daytime serials, frisking fawns more entertaining than game shows. A summer storm blowing in across the lake has the thrills of a hundred firework displays, a winter wind the sound of a dozen railroad trains. There's excitement in the return of the orioles in spring, motivation in the seed catalogs that arrive in season, reward in the vegetables frozen and canned as fall arrives. She would, essentially, be perfectly content to spend all of every day, forever, right here.

Maybe it's born in the blood and bred in the bone.

Scratch some of the most cosmopolitan people you know, find the farm boy or girl underneath, and chances are you'll twang a chord of nostalgia. They left the land for fame and fortune, true, but there seems to be a wistful echo in their words when they talk about the home place, a fondness for the life they lost.

Even now, as the cities and suburbs grow, and so-called "marginal farms" disappear, you watch the occupants of those farms walk away with sadness and regret. The lives they find may be more prosperous but the stars will be dimmer, the air thicker, the work without the same satisfactions. In a generation or two some whisper in the brain of a descendant may bring him or her back, looking for a piece of land, a creek, some trees. Perhaps the roads are heavy with recreation vehicles and the camping grounds filled with tents because most of our ancestors loved the soil and the travelers are trying to find their way home.

I know, now, that, fundamentally, that's what keeps us here.

For Alice it's been as natural and easy as the annual blooming of the daffodils. She's always known, but never stated, that, eventually, I'd come to my senses and answer that call from the country.

For me, five generations removed from any previous family agricultural enterprise, it is, still, a profound puzzlement. Oddly, I fight contentment tooth and nail. In my old trade and craft, hard-won skills earned considerable success, recognition, money, and totems like club memberships and company cars. At farming I'm an awkward apprentice, feeling my uncertain way. What money we gain from the land is laughable considering the time, work and effort required. We'll never get any Best of Show ribbons at the County Fair.

Those things shouldn't matter, but reflexes learned during thirty years of competitive endeavor die hard. One seeks reassurance of worth in the things one does well.

Hoping for reward and recognition, I write the books. They go the rounds of agents and publishers and return, unappreciated and without acclaim.

So I go back to the business arena as a freelance and consultant. In occasional jousts with marketing and advertising puzzles and problems I can, again, prove my mettle. But there's not the duress of regular reporting, the politics of any organization, the need to advance in a system. From those things we have declared independence and the declaration has held.

Another marvelous way to maintain contact with my old world, without returning to it, came my way, miraculously. A nearby university offered me the chance to teach the skills that I had learned and practiced in business. Nothing can more enhance a sense of worth than discovering that the experience and knowledge gained in earning a living is both desirable and transferable.

Alice watches my return to business and the move into teaching with patience and some amusement. She knows it's either that or an unreasonable restlessness unassuaged by this loveliest of places. Marty, my farming partner, wonders that I don't use more days for fishing, hunting, walking the woods. Off on my self-appointed rounds, I'm much less of a help to him in fence maintenance, cattle feeding, and other chores than I was a few years ago.

Maybe, someday, the tended acres, sleek cattle, weeded garden will be enough. Maybe, then, I can drift down the lake in the rowboat, waiting for the line to tauten, and think of nothing else.

It's a nice prospect, pretty as a rainbow's end, and just as hard for me to reach.

Alice, however, is already there.

ALICE:

At least, I'm close.

I know that Ken's found a life here that's far more satisfying than anything he's had before, that he's prouder of this home than of any other place we've ever lived, and that he understands, more than ever, how I feel about the country. Reluctantly, he's learning to share my feelings. He's been so conditioned to work and reward all of his life that he's slow to grasp the bounty that costs nothing but time and attention.

I can't help but contrast him to my dad, the true farmer. He worked with nature as a partner, not an adversary, never fretted at the weather and saw beautiful things in the middle of the hardest kind of work. Two days of rain in the middle of haying season and Ken is ready to sell.

Daddy was a whistler. When he started for the barn at 4:00 A.M. I could hear, from the snugness of my bed, his whistled, tuneful greeting to the day. He'd come in, after dark, his clothes dusty with wheat chaff, dark with sweat, and he'd be carrying some wild posies he'd found along the way. The three hundred and forty acres he tended comprised all the world he wanted, the seventy or so cows all the responsibility he needed, the bi-monthly milk checks all the compensation he required from the outside world. He experimented endlessly, raised sheep and sheared them, established hives and sold honey, planted an orchard and peddled fruit, delivered papers to the neighbors, built a goldfish pond in the backyard.

The barn was really his favorite place. All the symphony he needed was the milker motor humming, the rhythmic sucking sound of the cups on the cows' teats, the splash of milk into the buckets.

The only time he left the farm for more than twenty-four hours was when he was hospitalized for pneumonia, and the time he came to visit us in our first home. He came, wearing a cast and carrying a cane, because a horse had fallen with him and broken his leg. Otherwise he'd have stayed home!

Whether my fervent belief that happiness lies in closeness to the land is in the genes or comes from simple observation I'll never know. But I've always wanted my husband and children and grandchildren to share in such happiness. It is available.

After twenty years here, at Aurohn Lake, I think Ken is beginning to grasp the possibilities.

KEN:

I am. Meanwhile, she helps. Because the place where I teach is fifty miles distant and winter roads are treacherous, she agrees to spend three days a week in rented quarters away from home in winter months. When we come back to the lake, on Thursday evenings, it's as thrilling as were our first weekend visits to our new land.

It will be a happy day for her when I acknowledge the ultimate truth of some wisdom uttered by a dear, old friend, Leo Maginn. He was a mentor when I was young, a friend until he left this earth. He knew my talents, my ambitions and efforts, had watched my whole careeer with a paternal eye.

In his late eighties he came to visit Aurohn Lake, strolled the lawn, gazed at the hills, watched clouds reflecting in the water. He didn't talk a lot, was ruminative as he puffed a good cigar. When it was time for adieus, he stood on the terraced steps looking into some immense distance and said to me, softly:

"You've had some wonderful titles, my boy. Creative Director, that's an imposing one, Executive Vice-President sounds good, too. Fine, fine. But, as far as I'm concerned, this is the *only* really creative thing you've ever done."

Words to ponder.

They sing in my mind, now, when I bend and crouch and plant a row of garden corn. They make easier the stacking of logs against winter. They reassure as we contemplate the future.

So many friends have followed the golden retirement road to Sun City or Sarasota, to clusters and communes where abundant cash is the common bond. They write of wondrous golf courses, lives of silken ease in sumptuous condominiums. They express astonishment at our exile, the solitude we've sought. Some send letters from faraway places as they jet to new adventures in a constant round of travel. Admittedly, it all sounds inviting. Those who come to visit worry about what will happen "when you get older and can't handle all the work." I point out that we won't need as big a lawn, as productive a garden, that the herd, while rewarding, is not a necessity.

We're staying. What better place for the city boy and country girl to sort old photographs, bring order to the papers and letters and memories of a lifetime? It will be warm by the wood stove, there are plenty of filled jars in the fruit cellar.

Should there be no smoke coming from our chimney, good neighbors will stop to see why.

Meet the Authors

KENSINGER JONES

A native of St. Louis, Missouri, he began his writing career at the age of 10, doing skits for his Cub pack. After Army service overseas during World War II, he became the writer of an award-winning series of radio shows entitled, "The Land We Live In." His involvement in advertising took him from the Gardner Agency in his home town, to Chicago's Leo Burnett Company, to Detroit's Campbell–Ewald, and back to executive creative responsibilities for Burnett in Chicago, Sydney (Australia) and Singapore. Since becoming a countryman he has done consulting work for agencies and advertisers in Battle Creek, Kalamazoo, Grand Rapids and Lansing. From 1982 until the present he has been a Lecturer in the advertising department of Michigan State University. He is listed in *Who's Who in America* and *Who's Who in the World*.

ALICE GUSEMAN JONES

After growing up on a dairy farm near Grindstone, Pennsylvania, she graduated from that state's Clarion University with a degree in library science. When her two children, Jeffrey and Janice, were in high school, she earned her Master's at Wayne State University and promptly went to work in their school library. Since returning to country living she has served as a library cart volunteer at Pennock Hospital in Hastings and was a charter member of the American Association of University Women there. As a reader for the Services for the Blind and Physically Handicapped, Library of Michigan, she has recorded more than a score of novels, textbooks, legal documents, biographies, and requested volumes. The tapes are utilized throughout Michigan and are made available, nationally, by the Library of Congress. While a resident of Australia, and during extensive tours abroad, she wrote a column for local papers called "Alice's Crazy Quilt World."

Wilderness Adventure Books
320 Garden Lane P. O. Box 968
Fowlerville, MI 48836

Please send me:

_____ hardcover copies of *A CALL FROM THE COUNTRY* at $16.95

_____ paperback copies of *A CALL FROM THE COUNTRY* at $11.95

(Postage and sales tax will be paid by the publisher.)

I am enclosing $ _____ (send check or money order)

Mr./Mrs./Ms. _____

Street _____

City _____ State/Province _____ ZIP _____